West Academic Publishing's Law School Advisory Board

the Bar Exam's Multistate Essay Examination (MEE)

Suzanne Darrow-Kleinhaus

Professor of Law
Director of Academic Development and Bar Programs
Touro College
Jacob D. Fuchsberg Law Center

Irene McDermott Crisci

Interim Library Director and Head of Public Services
Touro College
Jacob D. Fuchsberg Law Center

A SHORT & HAPPY GUIDE® SERIES

WEST
ACADEMIC
PUBLISHING

a short & happy guide series is a trademark registered in the U.S. Patent and Trademark Office.

© 2019 LEG, Inc. d/b/a West Academic

    444 Cedar Street, Suite 700
    St. Paul, MN 55101
    1-877-888-1330

Printed in the United States of America

ISBN: 978-1-68328-857-2

To our students, who never fail to amaze us with their compassion, intellect, and heart.

Table of Contents

A Short & Happy Guide to the Bar Exam's Multistate Essay Examination (MEE)

CHAPTER 1

MEE Basics

A. What This Book Will Do for You

Lots of books have been written about the bar exam but not one has been written solely about the Multistate Essay Examination ("MEE"). And there really wasn't a need for another bar exam book unless it was going to give you something that was not available anywhere else. This book does exactly that: it gives you a one-source resource for what you need to maximize your performance on the MEE—not a generic essay writing guide, but a treasury of information, issue identification, and subject area frameworks tailored specifically for the MEE.

Having said that, this book is not intended to replace a bar review course. A course is essential for providing all the substantive law you need to know to pass the bar exam. Such courses are carefully constructed to give you the black letter law in all the areas of law that might be tested. This is a prodigious effort and best left to the professionals. Don't try to do this on your own.

Still, a bar review course does not teach you how to turn the law into point-worthy essays. A course gives you the substance of the law but not the process of legal analysis. It assumes you developed this skill in law school. Moreover, a bar review course does not show you how to turn an overwhelming amount of black letter law into something you can actually remember and use to write rule paragraphs in answering essays.

This is where we come in. We show you how to balance the need for memorization with the need for application. Since you must do both to succeed on the bar exam, we tell you how to manage your time and the materials so that you can do both. We teach you everything that you need to know about preparing for and taking the MEE to achieve the highest possible essay scores, including:

- How to use the individual Subject Charts and Table of Issues (charts, organized by MEE subject, that identify every issue and sub-issue tested on the MEE over the past 14 years) to see the frequency of tested topics and gain familiarity with how they are tested.

- How to de-construct an MEE question into its component parts.

- How to "Follow the Yellow Brick Road" to write a well-organized answer.

- How to recognize the "clues" in the bar examiners' specific use of language to lead you to the issue and the rule.

- How to write a solid analysis including every relevant fact by matching rule to fact using our Rule/Fact chart and unique "X's and O's" approach.

- How to answer an MEE question in 30 minutes by following our "Read one, Write one, Drill One" preparation process.

- How to perform "forensic IRAC" on your own thought process so that you can identify the flaws in your legal reasoning and correct them.

- How to apply "best practices" to memorize the black letter law.

- How to structure your study time by the day, the week, and the task throughout the bar review period to ensure adequate coverage of every topic and how it is tested.

B. MEE Format and Subject Areas

The MEE is administered by participating jurisdictions on the state day of their bar exam and consists of six 30-minute essay questions.[1] MEE questions are developed by the National Conference of Bar Examiners ("NCBE"), the entity that develops the licensing tests used by most U.S. jurisdictions for bar admission. These exams include the Multistate Bar Examination ("MBE"), the Multistate Performance Test ("MPT"), the Multistate Professional Responsibility Test ("MPRE") and, of course, the Uniform Bar Examination ("UBE").

Each jurisdiction sets the format for its bar exam and relative weight given to each section in calculating a bar passage score and makes this information available to candidates—unless it is a UBE jurisdiction where the weighting of each section is prescribed (the MBE is weighted 50%, the MEE 30%, and the MPT 20%). To this extent, each state's bar exam is unique and you'll want to know everything there is to know about the make-up of your particular bar exam. You should check your individual jurisdiction's scoring policies very carefully for how it weights each section of the bar exam in

---

[1] *See* National Conference of Bar Examiners, http://www.ncbex.org/exams/mee/preparing/ (last visited July 16, 2018).

calculating a passing score. A regularly updated list of each jurisdiction's bar admission office address and phone number is available from NCBE's website.

If you are not taking the UBE where the MEE is the essay component of your bar exam, then you must check with your jurisdiction to find out whether it administers the MEE or drafts its own state-essays or uses a combination of both. Also, you'll want to know whether you are to apply general principles of law or state-specific law in answering the MEE questions if they are used. Candidates taking the Uniform Bar Exam (UBE) "must answer questions according to generally accepted fundamental legal principles."[2]

MEE questions may include issues in more than one area of law. For example, Conflict of Laws issues may appear together with Civil Procedure, Family Law, or Torts. The specific areas covered vary from administration to administration and may include the following:

- Business Associations (Agency and Partnership; Corporations and Limited Liability Companies)

- Civil Procedure

- Conflict of Laws

- Constitutional Law

- Contracts (including Article 2 Sales of the Uniform Commercial Code)

- Criminal Law and Procedure

- Evidence

- Family Law

---

[2] *See* National Conference of Bar Examiners, http://www.ncbex.org/pdf viewer/?file=%2Fdmsdocument%2F25 (last visited April 12, 2018).

- Real Property

- Secured Transactions (Article 9 of the Uniform Commercial Code)

- Torts

- Trusts and Estates (Decedents' Estates; Trusts and Future Interests)

C. The Table of Issues and Individual Subject Charts

Every issue tested on the MEE for the past fourteen (14) years is identified and organized by subject area and exam administration in the Charts in this book's Appendix. When you correlate the Table of Issues with the Bar Examiner's MEE Subject Matter Outlines, you can see which topics and sub-topics have been tested—and how frequently. This allows you to focus your studies by concentrating on what has been tested and how it has been tested.

Ultimately, there is no way to predict what will be on the bar exam. However, the frequency of some issues and the benefit of gaining familiarity with the structure and content of past questions is excellent preparation to guide you through answering questions on new issues. MEE questions are generally consistent from one exam administration to another when it comes to their structure, use of language, length, and content. *While there is a strong likelihood that previously untested or infrequently tested topics will appear on each new administration of the exam, preparation by studying from past exams is nonetheless invaluable.*

D. What Is Required of You

The goal of the bar examiners is to test your competency for the practice of law. To pass the bar exam, you must demonstrate a firm grasp of the "black letter law" and a solid grounding in basic analytical, reading, and writing skills.

Having said this, the MEEs test these skills in very specific ways and we provide strategies for each of them. These skills include:

- Problem solving

- Reading comprehension

- Organizing information

- Identifying and formulating legal issues [whether, when]

- Writing a solid analysis

- Managing time efficiently

All of these are "practical" skills yet too many students spend most, if not all, of their bar prep time studying only the substantive law. Success on the bar exam requires mastery of both.

1. Study Actively

Studying for the bar exam requires "active" studying. Unfortunately, it is all too easy to assume a very passive role—sitting through your bar review course for four or more hours each day and then rereading your notes for another four hours. Before you know it, the day is over, you are exhausted, and you have not worked through a single question!

While your bar review course will provide a study schedule that factors in practice time with essays—and even writing out a few for submission to their graders—our experience has shown that it is not enough for most students. Just imagine going to take your road test and never doing more than read the driver's manual and drive the car around the block a few times. Well, going into the bar exam without doing several dozen essays will leave you in the same place: without the license you want.

We show you how to customize a study schedule that works just for you based on how and when you learn most effectively. We also show you how to structure your tasks by the day and by the week to ensure that you cover every subject a sufficient number of times before the bar exam. If you follow the structured study schedules diligently, you will have practiced a sufficient number of questions and under timed conditions to make the essay portion of your bar exam feel like just another study session. You will know exactly what to do and how to do it because you will have done it so many times before.

2. *Work with Past MEEs*

Released exams are your primary source for practice essays. All of the examples, strategies, and guidelines presented in this book are based on actual, released MEEs. While your bar review course includes a good number of simulated practice tests and essay writing exercises, there is no substitute for the real thing. Nor is there any need—not when NCBE and many jurisdictions make past exam questions available to you from their websites.

NCBE provides its own Analyses Sheets for each MEE. The Analyses Sheets are provided to the user jurisdictions to assist graders in scoring the candidate's MEE answers. They identify and explain all the legal and factual issues the drafters intended to raise in the questions. Notes to the graders also identify where candidates might be given credit for alternative arguments—and where they should not. While essential to graders, this information is invaluable to candidates in their preparation.

Some jurisdictions provide sample answers, either student essays or suggested analyses. If the jurisdiction provides candidate answers, then it is important to note that the answer is not perfect and should not be used for "the truth of the matter asserted" but rather, to get a sense of what an above-average candidate answer looks like. This shows that the bar examiners do not expect perfection, but do expect a well-reasoned analysis that is responsive to the question.

It is impossible to overemphasize the value of working from released bar exam questions. There is no greater authority on the bar exam than the writers and graders of the exam themselves and when they provide their questions and answers, they are doing what they can to make the test process as transparent as possible.

3. *Let Go of Your Notes*

The most effective way to learn the law the way you need to know it is to practice the problems. Instead of reading and rereading your notes, you need to do the questions to learn how the rules work. In short, you have to let go of your notes to learn the law. You will go back to your notes to help you work through a question, but in this way, your brain is doing the thinking and your notes are playing a supporting role—instead of the other way around.

We provide the plans and strategies you need to turn each study hour into an active learning experience. We show you how to learn the rules in the context in which they will be tested. It is not enough to memorize elements and rules without some idea of how they present in a problem. As you will see, the very best way to learn the rules in a way you can remember them is to practice them in the context of questions. In addition to learning the law, practicing questions is essential for developing your analytical, reading, and writing skills.

CHAPTER 2

Learning the Black Letter Law

A. How to Study for the MEE

The key to success is to have a study plan that puts you in control of your time and the material. However, before you can define your study schedule, it's important to know "what" and "how" to study for the bar exam.

First, you need to internalize the law. A solid knowledge of the black letter law is required for bar passage. You need to know the law to distinguish between the answer choices on the MBE and you need to be able to articulate the law to answer the MEEs. Preparing for the bar exam simply by attending lectures and reading through bar review outlines, even if read several times, does not allow for the type of internalization of the material necessary to respond to these questions. "Knowing the law" means that you internalize the material in such a way that you truly "own" it. This is not the same as thinking you know something because a term or concept seems familiar. There's a big difference between recognizing something because you've seen it before and really knowing it so that you can write it. The MEE requires you to know the rules with precision and specificity—and to be able to articulate them.

Second, you must sharpen your basic analytical, reading, and writing skills. You can easily fall into the trap of devoting all your time and energy to memorizing rules without ever developing your practical sense of how the law works. You'll be amazed at how many answers to questions depend as much on your understanding of general legal principles as on your knowledge of specific rules. This requires that you actively engage in the process by working through dozens of MEEs. Yes, we wrote "dozens"—this was not a typographical error. You need to do as many questions as possible to really learn the rules by working with them in a factual context. There is no substitute for this part of your preparation.

1. *Memorizing the Law*

Memorization is essential to success on the bar exam. As you proceed through your bar review course, make it a priority to memorize basic definitions and the elements of rules.

Whether answering questions on the MBE or the MEE, you need to know the law to see the issues in the facts and answer the questions. As we'll discuss in a subsequent section, the bar examiners are very careful in choosing their language in writing the questions so as to provide "clues" if you pay attention. Still, you need to know the rules so we're here to give you some suggestions on how commit the law to memory.

Here are some suggestions:

- Focus on basic vocabulary for each subject area.

- Create your own condensed study outline of key concepts in each subject area.

- Make your own flashcards.

  Remember when you were in grade school and had to learn the multiplication tables? You used flashcards and repeated the tables over and over again until you knew them cold. The same principle applies here.

- Create a short hypothetical for each rule.

  Play around with the facts of the hypothetical. Ask whether the change affects the outcome. Apply different rules to the same scenario. What if you apply the common law to this set of facts? What if you apply the majority rule? The minority rule? Same result or different result? This type of practice provides the context you need for understanding as well as remembering the rules.

- Whenever possible, "de-construct" a rule statement and reword it according to an "if, then, unless" construction. This lets you combine the general rule with the exception. It also provides a statement that you can remember because you wrote it and it is short.

  Examples:

  □ *If* a minor enters into a contract, *then* it is voidable at the minor's option, *unless* it is a contract for necessities.

  □ *If* a material mistake is made by both parties at the time the contract is made as to a basic assumption, *then* the contract is voidable by the adversely affected party, *unless* he bears the risk of the mistake.

☐   *If* a partner acts on behalf of the partnership, *then* the partnership is bound *unless* that act is beyond the usual or ordinary business of the partnership.

2.   *Subject Strategies*

Write rule statements for each subject's main and sub-issues as part of your studying. This lets you learn the law in a way that you can remember it because you've framed it in your own words. Building the paragraphs from the general rule to the exception and defining all legal terms of art allows you to pre-write large sections of your bar exam for the most frequently tested subject areas.

This process also "trains your brain" to think this way so that on the bar exam you will formulate such paragraphs for any area of law by working from what you know about how the law works. Consequently, you will no longer be paralyzed with fear of not remembering every word in your notes. You will "own the words" because you are their creator.

3.   *Don't Get Lost in the Details*

One of our students expressed a very common concern and one we need to discuss. It was a paralyzing fear of never being able to know what she thought would be "enough law"—and that even if she could remember the law, she would never know it as perfectly as she thought she should. She said, "If I don't have the right words in my head—the exact ones that I have in my notes from bar review—then I can't write an answer!"

This kind of thinking is dangerous and self-destructive. It prevents you from doing what you need to do. It is indeed possible to get lost in the details and lose sight of the big picture. And for many of you, the most challenging part of studying for the bar exam will be dealing with the tremendous volume of material from your bar review course. Between the notes you take in class and all the other study materials, there is an overwhelming amount of law to learn. And you must learn it. The problem is that you will try to memorize it in the very words in which it is presented to you and you will not be able to do so. This will lead to incredible frustration. And with good reason. You are trying to do the impossible. *You cannot expect to memorize every sentence of your notes.* Don't even try. That's because the material is not given to you in a form that you *can* remember. It is your job to craft it into sensible statements of law that you can remember and use to write the rule sections of essays. We'll talk about writing rule paragraphs in the chapter on essay writing, but for now, you need to know that a good part of studying for the essay portion of the bar exam will involve creating "rule statements" for as many of the tested issues as possible. You will build them into "paragraphs of law" as needed based on the specific facts of your problem.

B. The Who, What, and When of Practicing Questions

Studying to learn the material is one activity; practicing with it is quite another. Memorizing rules from flash cards and outlines won't guarantee that you'll recognize them when they're tested in a fact pattern. Instead, you must learn the rules in the context in which they're likely to appear.

There is a method to learning from practice exams and you may be surprised to discover that it's not just about sitting down and answering the questions. That's what you'll do on bar exam day but not when you're studying. The difference is between answering the questions and using the questions to learn.

One of the most important things you can keep in mind as you study is that the only test that counts is the one you take on exam day. All the rest is preparation.

1. *Whose Questions to Practice*

Just as you studied from your professor's old exams to prepare for law school finals, you'll review released MEEs from NCBE when you study for the bar exam. While your bar review course includes a good number of simulated practice tests and essay writing exercises, there is no substitute for the real thing. It is essential that you become familiar with the structure, style, and content of the questions you can expect to see on bar day. Since the ultimate authority on the bar exam are the bar examiners, their questions should be your primary source for practice questions.

2. *What Questions to Practice*

While you must practice questions in all of the MEE subjects, you can focus your energies in two ways: where you need the most work and where it will do you the most good. How do you know which subjects require the most work? All subjects are not created equal—not with the bar exam and not with you. By now, you should have a pretty good idea of your subject strengths and weaknesses. If you excelled in certain subjects in law school, it's likely to be the same on the bar exam. Here's where you can "save" some study time and "spend" it on the more challenging subjects.

3. *When to Practice Questions*

You should begin practicing exam questions as soon as you begin your bar review class. Don't make the mistake of waiting until you think you know enough law: first, you'll never think you know enough law; second, once you've attended or listened to a bar review lecture, and reviewed your notes on a topic, you're ready to get to work. Working with rules as you learn them by applying them in the context of new factual situations is the most effective way to learn whether you truly understand them. Now is when you look up answers to the questions that naturally arise as you practice the material.

4. *Why to Practice Questions*

The reason to practice questions is to learn from them. While you may find this difficult to believe, *you've learned as much as you are going to learn from your notes after you've read them once or twice*. You've got to put them aside and move on to the questions to apply what you've learned to actual problems. This is the only way to find out what you know and what you don't. When your studying is "question-driven," it will lead you back to any gaps in your knowledge of the rules.

Studying involves two distinct processes: one is learning the black letter law and the other is learning the reasoning process of applying law to facts. You must know how to reason through a question. Unless you practice the rules in the context of problems, you will not learn the reasoning process so essential to answering questions correctly. What you need to do is *learn how to learn* from the questions.

How do you learn from "doing questions"?

- By looking up the rule to help you work through analysis of a question: this is learning the rule in context for long-term memory retention.

- By going back to your outline and reviewing your notes to help you write an essay answer: this is repetition and reinforcement of the rule—as well as learning in context.

The next step is the "how" of doing questions.

C. Applying the Process

Now we get to the real work—how to study. This phase involves the sequence and method of studying for success on the MEE.

1. Sequence the Material

The following study sequence is designed to maximize your learning by providing a foundation for the MEE through the MBE. The black letter law that you need to answer MBE questions is the same law that you need for the seven MBE subjects on the MEE. By first working through MBE questions and learning the law in that subject, you can then apply it to writing an essay, allowing you to transfer and reinforce knowledge between different test modalities. Answering an MBE question requires that you know the law to recognize it when it presents as an answer choice whereas writing an essay requires that you know the law by summoning it forth from your own head.

Proceed as follows:

a.   Go to the UBE Chart and look over the MBE column. It lists the seven MBE subjects. Number each subject from 1 to 7 according to the order that you take it up in your bar review course. For example, if your bar review course begins with Civil Procedure, then you will write "1" in the box before Civil Procedure. Number the remaining six MBE subjects accordingly.

b.   Assuming that Civil Procedure is your first bar review subject, after you complete your Civil Procedure lectures, work through at least 50 Civil Procedure MBE questions. As you answer each question, be sure to read the explanations for both the correct and incorrect answer choices. Where appropriate, write the rules on flashcards. Tailor your rule statements to the specific facts that trigger the rule so that you will remember it more easily.

c.   After you complete approximately 50 MBE questions in a subject, you are ready to proceed to MEEs in that area. Later, you will go back and work through many more MBE questions in that subject as part of your overall bar prep, but now we are using the law that you've learned from the MBE as a foundation for writing MEEs.

d.   Now you are ready to apply the "Rule of Three" for mastering the MEE: Read one, Write one, Drill One. Select three MEEs from the appropriate Subject Matter Outline, making sure to choose three that deal with the same general topic. Refer to the next section, "Target the Topics", for guidance in selecting your essays.

e.   Work through the three selected MEEs according to the steps for outlining and writing MEEs in Chapter 3. The following is a summary of the steps:

•   Read and outline one.

Follow the process for reading and marking up the question. Take your time and pay attention to the language and structure of the question. Use the Rule/Fact chart to note the rules and facts that you would discuss. After completing your analysis, review NCBE's Analyses Sheets carefully, comparing their issues, rule statements, and analysis to yours. Identify where you were correct and where incorrect. Understand why.

- Write one (with notes if necessary, but not timed).

  Follow the process for reading and marking the question. Look up the law if you are not sure of it and write your answer. Compare your answer to the Analyses Sheets and proceed as outlined above.

- Drill one (under timed conditions).

  Answer the third MEE under timed conditions. Compare to the Analyses Sheets.

f.   After you've completed a set of three MEEs, you are ready to take up the next subject. Follow this process for each of the seven MBE subjects—first the MBEs in the subject, and then the MEEs.

g.   When you've covered the MBE subjects, move on to the other MEE subjects. Go to the UBE Chart once again and look over the MEE column where you will find the remaining MEE subjects. Number them in sequence according to how you've taken them up in your bar review course. Apply the Rule of Three to each subject.

h.   After you've completed the Rule of Three for each of the MEE subjects, go back to each subject and work through additional rounds. You can follow the Rule of Three or break it up as necessary based on your specific needs. For example, you might wish to "Read 1" and "Drill 2" because working under timed conditions is your specific weakness. On the other hand, if writing and timing are your strengths, they you will want to spend more time reading and outlining the questions so that you cover the field.

2. Target the Topic

Here's where you use the individual Subject Charts to select your essays. It is just as important to target what you study as it is to order the sequence in which you study. For example, when you are ready to practice MEEs in Civil Procedure, go to the Civil Procedure Subject Chart and peruse the listings. Each MEE is identified by exam administration and the specific issues tested on that particular Civil Procedure question. This detailed level of issue-specificity allows you to target your studies. Select three MEEs that cover personal and subject matter jurisdiction. There are many of them. While each question varies factually and by sub-issues, you will get solid coverage on the topic from completing MEEs according to the Rule of Three.

Some subjects, however, require several iterations of the Rule of Three to cover the scope of that subject adequately. This is because the subject provides several distinct and "test worthy" areas. For example, in addition to personal and subject matter jurisdiction, Civil Procedure questions frequently test motion practice, discovery, and appeals issues. Thorough preparation requires practice in all of these areas. Similarly, Family Law questions fall into distinct areas: pre-marital, marital, and separation issues, divorce and property issues, and child support and custody issues.

While individuals can vary in how many questions they need to review before feeling comfortable with a topic, consider the following subjects as requiring multiple applications of the Rule of Three:

- Civil Procedure
- Family Law
- Agency and Partnerships

- Corporations ad LLCs

- Criminal Law/Criminal Procedure

- Trusts and Estates: Decedent's Estates

- Trusts and Estates: Trusts and Future Interests

3. *Repeat the Process*

After you've completed a review of the MBE subjects as outlined above, go to the UBE Chart and number the remaining MEE subjects in the order in which you plan to take them up. Follow the Rule of Three for working through questions in each subject.

Note: Although preparing for the MEE is the primary focus of this book, we include reference to the MBE and the MPT in the schedules to ensure a comprehensive study guide.

UBE Chart

MBE	MEE	MPT
50% of score	30% of score	20% of score
200 questions: 175 scored 25 scored in each subject	6 essays = 30 minutes each	2 MPTs = 90 minutes each
☐ Civil Procedure	Possible essay topics include all MBE subjects plus the following below:	☐ Single MPT in 90 Minutes
☐ Constitutional Law	☐ Business Associations: Agency and Partnership	☐ Single MPT in 90 Minutes
☐ Contracts	☐ Business Associations: Corporations and LLCs	☐ Single MPT in 90 minutes
☐ Criminal Law	☐ Conflict of Laws	☐ Two MPTs in 3 hours
☐ Evidence	☐ Family Law	☐ Two MPTs in 3 hours
☐ Property	☐ Secured Transactions	
☐ Torts	☐ Trusts and Estates: Decedent's Estates	
	☐ Trusts and Estates: Trusts and Future Interests	

D. Structured Study Schedules

The objective is to define a workable routine and maintain it while allowing for flexibility based on changes during the bar review period. Although it may seem as if every day is the same day as in the movie *Groundhog Day*, it's not. Most of the first four weeks are spent in lectures, reviewing and making notes, and practicing questions while the final weeks are devoted to active study and memorization. And even within these periods, it's critical to mix up the activities so that you stay alert and focused.

Use the following schedules to help you set a realistic work schedule that allows for lecture time, review time, and practice time. You will want to set both a daily and weekly schedule so you can plan your time and your tasks.

It is important to note that the provided schedules are just samples: it is up to you to personalize them according to your needs. Still, there are some things that you need to keep in mind when you make changes. First, and perhaps most important, you must begin your studies each day at 9:00 a.m. because this is when you will take the bar exam. Some of you may need to acclimate to being wide awake this early in the morning! Second, you should include particular study practices that have worked for you in the past—if creating flowcharts helped you organize and remember the law, then include this activity in your schedule. Remember—this is your schedule. It has to work for you. Finally, you need to be kind to yourself and schedule regular time off. It will be difficult to give yourself permission to take time away from your studies, but it is essential to your well-being and the learning process itself. "Time off" can be one afternoon a week for three or four hours—enough time to take in a movie and dinner with a friend and just enough time to give you a meaningful break. It's important to schedule short "time outs" for an evening or afternoon every week so that you get a change of scenery and chance to regain perspective.

1. *By the Day*

Daily Study Schedule 1 covers the weeks during your bar review course. It assumes that you are taking your bar review course in the morning, so if you are taking your course at another time, make the appropriate schedule changes.

Daily Study Schedule 2 covers the post-lecture period. Once you've completed your bar review lectures, change your schedule to make practicing questions—MBE, MEE, and MPT—your priority.

Daily Study Schedule 1

Time	Activity
7:30-9:00	[Exercise], shower, breakfast
9:00/9:30-12:30/1:30	Bar review lecture
1:30-2:00/2:15	Break/Lunch
2:00/2:15-5:00	Active Learning: • MBEs in selected topic • MEEs in selected topic • MPTs in selected task (memo, letter, brief, other)
5:00-5:30	Break/Snack
5:30-6:30	Complete flashcards/outlines on the law from the MBE/MEE subjects.
6:30-7:30	Break/Dinner
7:30-10:00	Mapping the rules: synthesis Review bar review notes and flashcards/10-15 MBE questions
10:00-11:00	End of workday

Daily Study Schedule 2

Time	Activity
7:30-9:00	[Exercise], shower, breakfast
9:00-11:30	MBE questions
11:30-1230	Break/Lunch
12:30-3:30	MEEs in selected topic or MPTs in selected task • Read and outline • Write an MEE or MPT • Take under timed conditions
3:30-4:00	Break/Snack
4:00-6:00	Review selected topics based on MEE performance: • By MBE or additional MEEs
6:00-7:00	Break/Dinner
7:00-10:00	Mapping the rules: synthesis
10:00-11:00	End of workday

2. By the Week

The Daily Study Schedule identifies what you do during each hour of your 12-14 hour study day, but the Weekly Study Schedule identifies what subjects you will cover during those hours.

3. Avoid Burnout and Boredom

If you found it difficult to maintain your focus for the typical law school two-week final exam period, then you will find the six-to-eight-week bar review period a true challenge.

Here's what to do:

- Maintain a realistic work schedule, one that allows for lecture time, review time, practice time, and relaxation time.

- Once you've decided on a time for your bar review lectures, stay with your choice. Avoid alternating sessions unless you must make up a missed session or find that it's just not working for you.

- If you find yourself losing momentum and stuck in a study rut, then it's time to make some revisions. Consider changing your study location. If you've been studying in the same spot in the library, you might consider moving to another floor in the library. Or you might try studying at home. Sometimes a change in venue works wonders.

- Consider varying the sequence of study activities. Go back to your schedule and mix things up. Instead of answering MBE questions in the morning, head straight to MEEs. See what works to keep you engaged. Don't be afraid to change it again the next week if it's not working. There is no one way to do this—the only way is the one that works for you.

Weekly Schedule

Week of: _____

Day	Study Subjects	Time/Task
Monday	Con Law	9:00-11:30: Con Law MBE 12:30-3:30: Con Law MEEs (3) Read 1 and check analysis Outline 1 and check analysis Write 1 and check analysis
	Property	4:00-6:00: Property MBE 7:00-9:30: Mapping the rules; review Property video*
Tuesday	Con Law	9:00-10:00: Con Law MEE Under timed conditions Review with Analyses sheets
	Property	10:30-11:30: Property MBE 12:30-3:30: Property MEEs (3) Read 1 and check analysis Outline 1 and check analysis Write 1 and check analysis 4:00-6:00: Con Law MBE 7:00-9:30: Mapping the rules
Wednesday	Secured Transactions	9:00-11:30: Secured Transactions MEEs (2) Read 1 and check analysis Outline 1 and check analysis Repeat with second MEE

	Contracts	12:30-3:30: MPTs in selected tasks (memo, letter, brief, other) 4:00-6:00: Contracts MBE Night off
Thursday	Contracts	9:00-11:30: Contracts MBE 12:30-3:00: Contracts MEEs (3) Read 1 and check analysis Outline 1 and check analysis Write 1 and check analysis
	Bus Orgs/ Corps	4:00-6:00: Bus Orgs/Corps MEE Read 1 and check analysis Outline 1 and check analysis 7:00-9:30: Mapping the rules
Friday	Bus Orgs/ Corp	9:00-11:30: Bus Orgs MEE (2) Write 1 untimed Write 1 timed Check analysis 12:30-3:30: MPT in selected tasks (memo, letter, brief, other)
	Torts	4:00-6:00: MBE Torts Night off**
Saturday	Crim Law	9:00-11:30: Criminal Law MBE
	Bus Orgs/ Agency	12:30-3:30: Agency/ Partnership MEEs: (3) Read 1 and check analysis

		Outline 1 and check analysis
		Write 1 and check analysis
		4:00-6:00: Crim Law MEE (2)
		Write 1 untimed
		Write 1 timed
		Check analysis
Sunday		Day off**

* Where appropriate, include re-watching subject area video from bar review course.

** Schedule an afternoon, day, or evening off according to your needs. No one is expected to work 14 hours a day for seven days a week for eight weeks of bar review. You need to assess your progress and ability to stay focused and adjust your schedule accordingly to maximize productivity.

CHAPTER 3

Writing for the MEE

A. Writing Is a Dialogue

Before we discuss specific strategies for writing successful bar exam essays, let's talk about writing in general: I'm sure a good number of you have been very successful in law school and a large part of that success can be credited to your ability to communicate effectively in writing. For you, doing well on the MEE will be a matter of gaining familiarity with the types of essays and their structure. But for those of you for whom essays posed a bit more of a challenge, we want you to know that you, too, can do well on bar exam essays. There is a method to scoring points and this is what we are going to share with you.

If you think about it, you'll realize that the essays are your **opportunity to converse** with the bar examiners. With every word you write, your goal is to tell the grader that you are prepared to take your place in the profession—that you are ready to meet with clients, analyze their problems, and represent them in court.

How do you convey this message? By using the **language of the law** in the format and structure of legal analysis. This is the only way to demonstrate your competency to join the bar. Presumably, after reading hundreds of cases, you sound something like a lawyer. When a grader reads your essay, there should be "a scintilla of evidence" to show that you've attended law school.

The written portion of your bar exam presents the greatest opportunity for you to influence your score because *you are the one in control of the question when you write.* Unlike the MBE where you have to match up your analysis of the problem to fit one of the answer choices, here you have some flexibility. While there are limits determined by the issues set up in the facts, you can take a slightly different path and still accrue significant points.

You can write your way to bar passage—especially when what you write represents a substantial portion of your overall score. The written portion is 50% of your score on the UBE and in many non-UBE jurisdictions.

B. De-constructing MEE Questions and Analyses

1. De-constructing the Questions

You might be wondering how "de-constructing a question" differs from "reading a question." Generally, your focus when reading a question is to determine what is required to answer it. You are concerned with the information relevant to your task— evaluating whether the defendant committed felony murder, whether the statement was admissible, whether a contract was formed, and so forth. This is especially true when you are reading a question during the bar exam itself. Since you are working under timed conditions, you read quickly, as you must. And in doing so, you might miss critical clues in the text if you were not attuned to looking for them—which is exactly what the process of "de-construction" will show you.

Your purpose in de-constructing a question is to analyze its organization and content for patterns and consistencies and to gain familiarity with its structure and language. *It's also to use the questions to help you learn the law in the context in which it is tested.* This takes slow and careful reading and develops the process that you will then use on bar day. In the *Instructions for Taking the MEE* which appears on the back cover of each test booklet, NCBE advises examinees to "[r]ead each fact situation very carefully and do not assume facts that are not given in the question."[1]

Careful reading and attention to detail lets you see:

- How issues present in the facts.

    As you found with law school exams, certain facts give rise to certain legal issues. The more essays you read, the more familiar you become with seeing causes of action in the context of the facts in which they arise.

- How bar examiners use language to signal issues and non-issues.

    With words, especially adverbs and adjectives:

    Bar examiners are incredibly efficient at using a single word or short phrase to convey enormous meaning. Only careful reading of the questions—lots and lots of questions—will allow you to recognize signal language. It's not that the words are unusual or buried in the text, but they are easy to overlook in the anxiety of taking the exam unless you know to look for them.

---

[1] *See* National Conference of Bar Examiners, http://www.ncbex.org/pdf viewer/?file=%2Fdmsdocument%2F25 (last visited June 29, 2018).

For example, consider the phrases "walking peacefully" and "without provocation or warning." Such phrases convey enormous meaning. Consider a Criminal Law problem where you're told the plaintiff was "walking peacefully" or the defendant acted "without provocation or warning." You'll know that a claim of self-defense is not viable because it is not grounded in the facts.

Another example of a loaded phrase is "public place." Just think of the possibilities for Property and Constitutional Law questions. Here two words can make all the difference in your analysis.

The same is true for such words as "written" and "oral" and all the possible phrases used to convey their meaning. Consider e-mails, telexes, and letters for writings; think of telephone conversations for oral discussions. These words figure prominently in Contracts and Property questions. Look for them.

Bar examiners are similarly adept at using language to signal non-issues. Only the careful reader will know not to discuss such matters, saving time and points for the real issues. For example, when the hypothetical contains such phrases as,

> *"Signed and duly acknowledged"*

> *"Proper written consent"*

> *"Duly executed"*

> *"Duly commenced"*

it's your signal *not* to discuss the matter. For example, if you are told that "the will was duly executed," then the issue is not a problem with one of the elements required for execution. Accept what the bar examiners are telling you and move on to address the real issue in the problem.

With declarative statements:

This one presents a bit differently but is equally important because it leads to an issue or an essential part of a claim. The MEE landscape is full of the following kinds of leading sentences. For example, when you come upon sentences like the following,

> *"No filings of any type were made in connection with the formation of Empire."* (Feb 2014, Agency, Partnership)

> *"Without conducting an environmental evaluation or preparing an environmental impact statement, the USFS approved a development project in the Scenic National Forest that required the clearing of 5,000 acres of old-growth forest."* (July 2014, Civ Pro)

> *"The agreements are silent as to the allocation of losses."* (July 2012, Corp)

Naturally, the first thing you think when you read such sentences is whether such filings are necessary, whether an environmental evaluation or impact statement is necessary before approval of a federal project, and what is the default for allocating losses when an LLC's operating agreement does not provide for them. Such statements appear frequently in MEE questions and the MBE as well. They are issue signals. Be sure to discuss them in your analysis.

- How the structure, length and format of fact patterns help you narrow your focus.

MEE questions tend to be five to seven paragraphs long where the final paragraph before the interrogatories typically identifies the parties' arguments or claims. This structure is incredibly helpful in focusing your attention and identifying the issues in controversy.

2. De-constructing the Analyses Sheets

The National Conference of Bar Examiners' Analyses Sheets are very helpful in your preparation for the MEE since they allow you to self-assess your work. They identify the issues you need to address in your answer, the rules of law, and the appropriate arguments. However, the Analyses Sheets are not written as "sample answers." Rather, they are intended for the bar examiners in the individual jurisdictions who are using the MEEs as part of their bar exam.

The Analyses Sheets provide guidance to the graders as to what should be in a candidate answer, suggestions on how to weight the issues, and additional notes as to what should be considered point-worthy and why. The Analyses Sheets also provide this invaluable guidance to you so be sure to include them in your study materials. When referencing the Analyses Sheets, however, you do not need to consider the references to cases, hornbooks, treatises, restatements, etc. These are not expected in a candidate answer but are citations to authority for the grader jurisdictions.

Individual jurisdictions may release candidate answers for the MEE. If your jurisdiction releases sample answers, be sure to review them carefully: they are not always correct on the law but are chosen as better than average answers and meant to be representative of what is generally expected in an answer.

Now that you have de-constructed exam questions, it's time to de-construct exam answers—an equally important part of your preparation. Here, rather than studying past exams to see what *you* can expect from the bar examiners, your goal is to learn what *they* expect from you.

By examining each part of a sample answer, you will learn:

- How important a statement of the issue is to the development of the answer.

- How much rule you need to write to address the issue.

- How a complete and concise statement of the rule differs from a treatise-like discussion.

- How analysis of the facts differs from a recitation of the facts.

In addition to observing the heavy dependence on IRAC construction, you will discover such other critical information as:

- The need to state the "obvious."

For example, in working with a Sales question, many a bar candidate neglects to make such a basic statement as

> *"This was a contract for the sales of goods because computers are goods."*

but such a sentence is essential to a solid analysis because it completes the nexus between your statement of law that the Uniform Commercial Code Article 2 governs transactions involving sales of goods and your facts which discuss the sale and delivery of some computers.

Equally obvious, equally necessary, but equally absent from too many answers is a reference to the controlling law

"Under the Fourth Amendment to the Constitution, a person has the right to be free from unreasonable searches and seizures. . . ."

"Under the Federal Rules of Evidence, hearsay is an out-of-court statement introduced in court to prove the truth of the matter asserted."

- The heavy reliance on signal language to lead the reader through the steps of an IRAC analysis.

"The issue is whether . . . . , *when* . . . . . ."

"Under the [identify the controlling law: common law, federal rule, statute etc.]"

"Here, the [buyer accepted the goods *because* . . . .]"

"Therefore, . . ."

- The use of "because," "since," "as," and "when" in the analysis section of the essay to connect rule with fact.

C. Follow a Formula: Write IRAC

It should be clear from the de-construction process that your answers will follow a basic IRAC structure and it's okay to be obvious about it. There's no need to worry that you're boring the grader. He or she will be very grateful to find the issue in your essay so easily. Also, there's no need to try and impress the grader with your originality. Save the sparkling prose and follow IRAC to proceed swiftly through your paces on the bar.

IRAC allows you to organize your response and remain in control, whether addressing a narrow issue-driven essay or a general question. IRAC is your blueprint for answering any MEE question.

This is where most books would leave you to your own devices. After describing the basics of IRAC, you'd be given some hypotheticals and told to practice the process by writing out answers. However, a vital piece in the process is still missing—that is, how to do it. It's one thing to tell you to write an answer—and quite another to show you how it's done. Sometimes, you need to be shown exactly what to do.

1. *Stating the Issue*

Identifying and then following the "issue" is essential to completing the MEE within the 30-minute time frame and achieving maximum points. Points are only awarded for discussion of the relevant law and analysis and faithful adherence to your issue assures that you will do this.

The challenge for most candidates is stating the issue. It is not, as you may think, the question that you are asked in the interrogatory. That's just a question and you must turn it into the issue by connecting the rule in controversy with facts that determine the outcome—the "operative facts."

Separate the tasks and avoid "brain freeze"

Now this is important: 99% of the time, you can identify the legal issue even if you are not 100% sure of the rule that answers it. ***Do not let uncertainty about the rule stop you from addressing the problem you see in the facts.*** Building the rule that addresses the issue is a separate task both mentally and logistically. When you are trying to find the issue, your concern is simply that: what is the legal problem? Even if you don't think you know the rule, you can still find the problem. Answering it is a separate task. Trying to do both at once leads to "brain freeze" and paralysis. Instead, take up only one thing at a time. This means that when you are trying to identify the issue, you're not also trying to state the rule and apply it to determine the outcome! By the time you get to stating the rule, you will find the words. You'll find the words because that's all you'll be focused on at that time.

Changing direction: from the facts to the rule

Finding the issue means that you let the facts in the problem speak to you. And they will if you practice as we've discussed. *It takes practice because you are used to studying from the rule to the facts and now you are being asked to think in the opposite direction—from the facts to the rule.* If you think about it, you will see why it takes time to switch your brain from one type of thinking to another: while you've been reading your outlines and listening to lectures, you've been focusing on "rule, rule, rule" but largely outside of the context of the facts that trigger them. Now you need to be able to identify from the facts what rules are implicated.

Here's why the conscientious application of the Rule of Three is so important. It gives you the practice you need in the way that you need it to see how the bar examiners plant clues in the language and present the facts in a certain way so as to elicit responses from you—if you've been paying attention.

When you have identified the issue, write it as simply and directly as possible. Begin your sentence with *"The issue is whether"*. It's okay to be obvious.

- *Use the "whether, when" construction.*

   The "whether, when" construction leads you to connect the legal question with the specific facts in controversy. When you use this approach to formulate an issue, you avoid overly general statements and provide a path to follow in your analysis. This leads to an essay that connects the rules with the questions presented rather than one that rambles and follows a "kitchen sink" approach.

Begin with,

> *"The issue is whether"*

then identify and state the legal conclusion you want the court to reach,

> Ben **committed a battery**, (or a **contract was formed**, or the **court can assert personal jurisdiction** over the non-resident defendant)

and connect to the facts in controversy which determine the outcome,

> **when** *he threw the vase at Amy and hit Jill (or* **when** *the acceptance contained additional terms, or* **when** *the defendant rented office space and opened a checking account in the forum state)*

You end up with the following issue statements

> *"The issue is* **whether** *Ben committed a battery* **when** *he threw the vase at Amy and hit Jill instead."*

> *"The issue is* **whether** *a contract was formed* **when** *the acceptance contained the additional term of charging interest on late payments."*

> *"The issue is* **whether** *the court can assert personal jurisdiction over the non-resident defendant* **when** *the defendant rented office space and opened a checking account in the forum state."*

2. Building the Rule of Law

After your identification of the issue, your statement of the law is essential. If you are taking the UBE, then you must answer questions according to generally accepted fundamental legal principles. If you are in a non-UBE jurisdiction, then you should still answer according to generally accepted legal principles unless your jurisdiction has instructed you to answer according to state and local law.

a.   Write Enough Rule

The major problem, and where candidates fail to get as many points as they can and should, is that they do not write enough law and they do not do so in a complete, concise, and coherent manner.

By now, we're sure that you're asking yourself:

- What is enough rule?

- How do I know how much rule to write?

- Isn't there such a thing as too much rule?

The answer is simple: the whole rule is enough rule to provide the context to analyze the facts. The rule and the facts are inextricably linked. Your analysis of the facts will not make sense unless you have first identified the rule which determines the relevance of those facts. You must use the facts of the problem to guide your discussion of the law—which also means that you will "build" a rule paragraph, sentence by sentence, as necessary.

b.   Write the Rule in Its Logical Order

There is a structure to follow when writing a rule of law. You should strive to present your statement of the law in its logical order, even if it does not come into your head this way. Typically, your thought process will not be this organized. It's far more likely you'll jump to the specific rule necessary to answer the issue in dispute—usually the exception—and forget to include the rest of the rule in your essay. Here's where an outline can help you build a complete rule paragraph. Please review the Rule Outline Worksheet to see how to outline the rule the way your mind thinks of it and then re-order it to its logical written order.

Writing the rule this way shows your understanding of the subject and makes it clear to the grader. Just as you need a context to make sense of what you hear—just imagine hearing only one side of a telephone conversation—a reader needs a context to understand what you write. You provide it as follows:

- Move from the general to the specific.

  There is a "natural" order to writing the rule which is based on a hierarchy of concepts. This means that when you write the rule, you work from the general to the specific. Your analysis should begin with a statement of the general rule and then move to the exception, not vice versa. The general rule provides a context for understanding and appreciating the role of the exception.

  For example, suppose your problem requires you to evaluate a challenge to a federal expenditure brought by a taxpayer and the question turns on whether the taxpayer has standing. Since the general rule is that a federal taxpayer lacks standing to raise a constitutional challenge to federal expenditures, then surely you are dealing with one of the exceptions. Consequently, before you identify the exception and evaluate its merits, you must preface the discussion with a statement of the general rule.

- By defining each legal term of art.

  When your statement of the rule contains a legal term of art, your next sentence should be a definition of that term. This is one of the easiest ways to go about building a complete statement of the rule in a logical and methodical manner. The sentences flow almost effortlessly because one statement leads naturally to the next.

- By using the following building blocks of rule construction.

Elements: even if you've identified a specific element of a rule as the one in controversy in your problem, you still need to include a general statement identifying all of the elements.

For example, suppose your issue is whether a party's possession of property was uninterrupted for the statutory period to satisfy a claim in adverse possession. While the heart of your analysis will be this question of continuous possession, you will preface your analysis with a general statement identifying the basic elements required for a cause of action in adverse possession: actual and exclusive possession, hostile to the true owner, notorious and open, and uninterrupted for the statutory period. Then you will focus on the element or elements in controversy. The point is that even though only one or two of the elements may be in dispute, you need to identify all of them to provide context. (While you will also need to offer a brief statement as to why they are not in dispute, this part will be addressed in the analysis section.)

Exceptions: exceptions to the general rule are the stuff of which bar exam essays are made. In fact, you can pretty much count on the questions to force you to deal with exceptions because that's where the problems typically arise in the real world.

Distinctions: often you will have a question where the state law differs from the federal rule or the common law from the statutory law. If appropriate for your jurisdiction, be sure to identify such distinctions to show how application of one rule as opposed to the other would yield a different result.

The following is a good example:

The common law's "mirror image rule" and UCC 2-207:

Under the common law, the "mirror image rule" requires that an acceptance conform exactly to the terms of the offer and any variation is deemed a counter-offer and terminates the offeree's power of acceptance. The result under the UCC 2-207 is radically different. Here, a contract for the sale of goods may be formed even if the acceptance "states terms additional to or different from those offered." 2-207(1). Consequently, in one case we have a contract whereas in the other we don't.

RULE OUTLINE WORKSHEET

After formulating the issue, ask yourself each question:

Step 1   What is the *specific rule* brought into controversy by the facts?

_____

_____

Are there *legal terms* of art to define?

_____

_____

Step 2   What is the *general rule*?

_____

_____

Build the general rule of law:

A.   Are there *legal terms* to define?

_____

_____

B.   Are there *exceptions* to the general rule?

_____

_____

C.   Are there *elements/factors* to be identified?

_____

_____

Step 3   Is there a *relevant distinction*?

(i.e., between the common law and the UCC or state law/between federal and state law?)

_____

_____

_____

Step 4   Does the party have a relevant *defense*? or is there a *limit* to the reach of the rule?

_____

_____

Step 5   What are the *consequences* of applying this rule to the facts?

       For example, should evidence be excluded under the *exclusionary rule*?

_____

_____

       Is the party entitled to damages? If so, what kind? Punitive? Economic? Equitable?

_____

_____

Step 6   Is there a *procedural element* to consider? A motion? What is the standard? (i.e., summary judgment)

_____

_____

3. *Writing the Analysis*

a. "Run the Rule": Application = Rule + Fact

The analysis portion of your essay is the heart of the discussion. Your job is to examine the legal significance of each fact in light of the rule. Every fact of consequence to the outcome should be in your analysis. These are the easiest points to get and the easiest to ignore because you're concerned about the rule.

The difficulty for many bar candidates is simply reciting the facts or ignoring them altogether. Yet this portion of the IRAC is the easiest of all because you've already done the heavy lifting by identifying the issue and writing the rule.

After writing the rule paragraph, you're ready to "run the rule." Running the rule means that you match up each part of your rule statement—element, factor, requirement—with its corresponding "fact" in the problem to see how it plays out.

How you set up the rule now drives the structure of the analysis. Your statement of the rule provides a blueprint to follow for your discussion of the facts. Work from your articulation of the rule to guide your application of the facts. Match up each element/factor you've identified in the rule with a fact, using the word "because" to make the connection between rule and fact. This ensures that you write facts "plus" the significance of those facts. Words like "since", "when", and "as" work just as well as "because."

Think of writing the application portion of your analysis in terms of a formula:

Application = Rule + Fact,

where "+" is "because"

(A = F + R)

Consider the following examples:

- Scarlett may have committed a "trespass" *(rule)* **because** (+) she "walked onto Farmer Dell's cornfield to pick corn without his permission" *(facts)*.

- Ted acted in "bad faith" *(rule)* **because** (+) he "counted on the good price he was paying for the raw materials when he decided to increase operations" *(facts)*.

- Sam the shareholder has a basis to "pierce the corporate veil: *(rule)* **because** (+) Lola was the "the sole shareholder and freely intermingled funds, used corporate funds to pay both corporate and personal expenses (her credit cards), maintained only one set of accounting books, and never held any corporate meetings" *(facts)*.

b. "The Fact Whisperer": Listen to All of the Facts

A hallmark of a solid analysis is one that identifies and addresses all the relevant facts and, especially, the ambiguities in the facts. That's the essence of analysis—seeing the possible ways to interpret the facts and then explaining the consequences that flow from each interpretation.

It's your job to look closely at the facts and let them speak to you. Virtually every fact in an MEE is there for a reason. It's your duty to ask: "Why is this fact here?" If you ask the question, you will find the reason, but you need to ask. *You need to see the meaning in the facts and if you are not actively looking at the facts and questioning them, you will not hear what they are telling you.*

Further, it's critical to keep an open mind with respect to the facts because "once you've concluded, you're precluded" from seeing the possibilities. If you've reached a conclusion immediately upon reading a fact, then you've shut down the possibility of seeing the facts in any other way—you've precluded the counter-argument.

Conclusion-driven thinking leads to conclusory statements because you have already determined the outcome. It prevents you from writing analysis. This means that you must keep an open mind beginning with your initial read of the facts. For example, when you're reading the problem and think you've spotted an issue, instead of writing: "breach", write: "breach?" Writing a question mark ("?") keeps the question open in your head to analysis.

Recognize, Identify, but no Need to Decide

If you find an ambiguity in the facts, confront it. Even if you don't know how it would be resolved legally, don't ignore it. Instead, embrace it: identify the problem and use the facts to explain why it's an issue. Outline the possibilities, but you don't have to resolve the problem—you just have to identify it.

Finally, think of the "A" in IRAC as not just "Analysis" or "Application" but as the "Accessories" in your discussion. Just as accessories add color, individuality and spark to your outfit, so, too, with using the facts in your essay. This is where you show how the rules connect with the facts to complete the picture. And like accessories, facts are usually the least expensive item in your wardrobe. Better yet, the "facts" are free—you don't have find them or create them as you do with the issue and the rule. You just have to use them. The facts are there for the taking and by doing so, you gain invaluable points.

4. *Stating the Conclusion*

A conclusion completes the "frame" to the question that is anchored on the other side by the issue statement. Sometimes, you may find that an ambiguity in the facts does not allow for a definitive answer. In that case, just say so. This is the heart of analysis. Explain what you see and why. What matters is not that you reach a conclusion but that you show the reasoning by which you reach your result.[2]

---

[2]   Once again, this is exactly what NCBE writes in it Instructions for Taking the MEE: "Each of your answers should show an understanding of the facts, a recognition of the issues included, a knowledge of the applicable principles of law, and the reasoning by which you arrive at your conclusions. The value of your answer depends not as much upon your conclusions as upon the presence and quality of the elements

If the call-of-the-question asks for a specific answer, then be definitive. State your conclusion as to that issue. If there are multiple issues, then once you've completed your analysis of one issue, move on to the next. And it's as simple as that—begin a new paragraph and write,

> *"The next question is whether Spence's offer was accepted when Ben said he'd take two cartons but delivery had to be September 15th, not the 20th."*

D. Automate the Process

One of the primary purposes of taking practice exams—and the whole basis for the Rule of Three—is to make the process of reading and answering the questions so routine that you'll follow it instinctively on exam day. *Your main focus will be on what you write, not how you write it.* Aside from allowing you to focus on substance, having a plan saves time and prevents panic because you know exactly what to do.

1. Allocate Your Time for Each Question and Set Your Timetable

You have 30 minutes for each MEE. On bar day, you will create your own "clock" by writing down the starting and ending times for each question. This way, all you have to do is look at the time and you know when to move on without having to make any calculations. You have already figured it out.

For example, if your MEE session begins at 1:30 p.m., then your clock looks like this:

---

mentioned above." *See* National Conference of Bar Examiners, http://www.ncbex. org/pdfviewer/?file=%2Fdmsdocument%2F25 (last visited June 29, 2018).

MEE 1   1:30-2:00

MEE 2   2:00-2:30

MEE 3   2:30-3:00

MEE 4   3:00-3:30

MEE 5   3:30-4:00

MEE 6   4:00-4:30

Follow this clock throughout the exam to stay on track. There is no borrowing time from one question for another. You need to keep moving forward to the next question at the end of each 30-minute period.

Budgeting your time and working within that time is the only way to ensure that you'll complete the exam—or come as close as possible. You begin working toward this goal the minute you start studying for the bar exam. Every practice essay is a dress rehearsal.

Timing for an Individual MEE

After you've written a number of MEEs under timed conditions, you will see that your reading/outlining/writing time breaks down similarly for each question. This is not something that you can schedule like the general clock of 30 minutes per MEE, but the breakdown of 30 minutes per each essay runs something like this:

First read: 2 minutes

Second read, notes and outline: 6-8 minutes

Write: 20 minutes

Average writing time: 4-5 minutes per issue

2. Scan the Exam but Answer the Questions in Order

You want to get a sense of the entire exam but it's usually best to simply follow the order of questions when answering them. If you start to read each question before deciding which one to answer, you'll waste precious minutes and dilute your concentration. Instead, take one at a time as you find them.

On the other hand, you need to be flexible. For example, suppose you begin a question and find that no matter how hard you try, you can't make any progress. You need to stop and move to the next question. You cannot afford to waste valuable time when you could be working productively elsewhere. Chances are that when you return to this question later, it will come to you.

3. Begin at the End of the Question with the Call-of-the-Question

The interrogatory or "call-of-the-question," lets you know what is required of you. This informs your subsequent reading of the fact pattern and ensures that you read actively for the information you need.

From the interrogatory, determine whether it's a "general" or "specific" style essay. A "general" style essay leaves the question open-ended. The following are some examples from past MEEs:

- "Is the landlord correct? Explain." (February 2013)

- "Did the board of directors properly approve the purchase of the asset? Explain." (February 2012)

- To whom should Testator's estate be distributed? Explain." (July 2017)

On the other hand, a "specific" essay presents a seemingly more precise question to be addressed.

- "Under the Fifth Amendment as applied to the states through the Fourteenth Amendment, is the city ordinance requiring the restaurant to install floodlights an unconstitutional taking? Explain." (February 2014)

- "Did the trustee breach any duties in acquiring and retaining the portfolio of mutual funds and, if yes, what remedies are available to the trust beneficiaries if they sue the trustee? Explain." (July 2015)

- "What type of LLC was created—member-managed or manager-managed? Explain." (July 2016)

What's interesting in both cases, whether a "general" or "specific"-type question, they are really the same when it comes to the MEE. This is because even when it's a general question, the MEE typically identifies the parties' claims in the paragraph(s) immediately preceding the question. And when it's a specific question, you still have to do the same work to connect up with the precise issue in controversy. It's just a matter of presentation and what you need to do to answer either form of the question is the same.

4. *Read the Entire Question for the First Time*

- Beginning with the call-of-the question, take approximately two (2) minutes to read through the question to determine the subject area and get a sense of the problem and the parties.

- Re-read the interrogatories. Set up your outline on your laptop as outlined in section 5, adding to it as appropriate.

As you read, note the following:

- Identify the area of law and the legal relationship of the parties: employer and employee, husband and wife, buyer and seller, landlord and tenant, etc., by writing the words. Relationships determine duties owed.

- Circle amounts of money, dates, locations, quantities, ages, words that go to "knowledge" and "intent", "public" and "private", etc. Circle the words in a bubble, like a big "O." This ensures that relevant facts pop out of the text so you don't miss them. We will get back to them later when writing the analysis.

- Look for and circle the words "oral" and "written" and the numerous variations that lead to the same result: he "phoned", he "called", "she sent an email", "she sent a fax."

- Identify issues by stating them and with a question mark: "merchants?", "excited utterance?", "anticipatory repudiation?", "breach?" Notice the question mark? This is critical: writing a question mark means that you are questioning whether this might be so, not concluding that it is. This ensures that you will keep your mind open so that you can see possible counter-arguments. *If you've already concluded when you've read something, then you're precluded from seeing the possibilities in the facts.*

5. *Outline Your Answer*

Resist the impulse to start writing immediately—it doesn't matter what others around you are doing—it's worth a few minutes to think through the problem and plan your response.

Instead, you're going to organize your ideas into an outline based on the relevant issues and the writing will flow from there. While this process is designed for those who type their answers, others can follow the principle on scrap paper without sacrificing time by sticking to buzz-words and phrases only.

There are two ways to outline, depending on whether the MEE has numbered questions or a general question. Outline your essay answer on your laptop as follows:

a. When Working with Numbered Questions in a Specific-Style Essay

- "Follow the Yellow Brick Road" by using the number for each question to set up your outline. This is the first step toward a well-organized answer because you are using the structure of the question to answer it. Type in the numbers skipping several spaces between them.

- For each number, identify the issue in controversy. Go back to the specific paragraph or paragraphs in the fact pattern that address that question and read carefully, letting the facts speak to you. Write the issue in the "whether, when" format whenever possible.

- Under the issue statement, write the rule(s) necessary to answer the issue. Bullet them. Don't worry about the order in which you will write them— just note them in the order that they come to you now. You will put them in their logical order when you write your analysis.

- Using bullet points, enter the relevant facts from the fact pattern under the rules. As you go through the relevant paragraph(s) for the facts, mark an "X" through each "O" when you've added it to your outline.

  If you see "O's" that have not been "X'd" out, then you must go back to the "O's" to see why you have not included them in your outline. You are probably missing facts that you need for your analysis. Every fact of consequence must be in your answer.

- Turn the bullet points into sentences, using the formula for creating analysis: "Here, X (relevant rule: made an offer to work for Café) because Y (relevant facts: it followed extensive negotiations between the parties, and contained definite terms—head pastry chef, for two years, for annual salary of $100,000."

b. When Working with a General-Style Essay

- Mark each paragraph by number.

- Read the first paragraph and see whether an issue presents in the facts. You may have to read on to the second paragraph, but by then, you will find your first issue.

- Proceed paragraph by paragraph. Identify and number the issues as you see them.

- Under each issue statement, write the rule(s) necessary to answer the issue. Bullet them. Don't worry about the order in which you write them—just note them in the order that they come to you. You will put them in their logical order when you write your analysis.

- Go back to each paragraph and identify the facts that are relevant to each issue. Using bullet points, enter the relevant facts from the fact pattern under the rules. As you go through the relevant paragraph(s) for the facts, mark an "X" through each "O" when you've added it to your outline.

    If you see "O's" that have not been "X'd" out, then you must go back to the "O's" to see why you have not included them in your outline. You are probably missing facts that you need for your analysis. Every fact of consequence must be in your answer.

- When you've completed your list, you may need to revise the sequence of issues into a logical order for your written analysis.

6. Write the Essay

Now that you've framed an outline based on the issues, rules, and facts, you're ready to write the essay. When you write, you'll follow your outline, referring to each issue and bulleted rules and corresponding facts. Your outline will lead you from one issue to the next as they naturally unfold. This process assures that your answer will be well-organized.

a. Follow the "Yellow Brick Road" and/or Use Sub-Headings

Once again, if your MEE has numbered interrogatories, you've used them to set up your outline and the numbers should be in your answer as well. The grader is looking for them. It shows that you follow directions and makes it easy for the grader to know which question you are addressing.

If the MEE is a general-style essay, you can use the numbers you set up in the outline or you can use sub-headings to keep organized. Your choice of sub-heading should be simple and direct. The names of parties and causes of actions are good choices. Consider the following:

Ben v. ABC Company

Buyer's Remedies

Molly's Defenses

b.   Write IRAC

Follow your outline and turn your notes into answers.

- Write each issue using the "whether, when" construction to combine the rule with the operative facts.

- Write your rule statement for each issue by working from the general to the specific and defining each legal term of art.

- Introduce your analysis with *"Here"* or *"In this case."*

- Match each rule with a "fact" using "because" to link the two. When you've finished your analysis, go back to the fact pattern and check to see that each "O" has been "X'ed" out. This ensures that you've actually referred to all the facts in your analysis.

- If you find an ambiguity in the facts, confront it. Even if you don't know how it would be resolved, don't ignore it. Instead, embrace it: identify the problem and explain the possibilities. You don't have to resolve the problem. You just have to identify it.

- Conclude and continue: offer a conclusion, even if only a "more likely than not", with respect to the issue and repeat the process where each issue forms the basis for a separate IRAC analysis.

7. *When 30 Minutes Are up, Move on to the Next Question*

Follow your schedule faithfully. You cannot "borrow" time from one question for another. This never works. Instead, you must move on. If you have time remaining when you've finished all of the questions, then you can go back.

Still, if you've typed your outline for the question as we've discussed, you already have the critical pieces in place—issue statement, rules, and facts—to get some points even if you haven't finished the analysis in a purely essay format.

E. "Be in the Moment"

No matter how much you've studied, how many practice exams you've taken, and how carefully you've outlined and considered what's likely to be tested, once you get to the exam, you must be prepared to let go and "be in the moment." This means that you respond to what the bar examiners ask of you and not what you want to tell them. The questions are carefully crafted to test you on certain material; if you turn the questions around or avoid answering them, you're thwarting their agenda and substituting your own. TRUST US—there's no better way to ensure a poor or even failing grade than to ignore what's asked of you. Answering the bar examiners' questions is the only way to show what you know.

Forget about "perfection" and just write. You are not writing for publication but bar passage. Think of the words from "Frozen" and "Let It Go." Keep writing until you write without thinking about how you are writing but what you are writing. You've studied long and hard: the process will take over.

F. Other Essay Writing Strategies

1. Write in Paragraph Form

You would be surprised how many candidates forget how to use paragraphs and write in a stream of consciousness style worthy of William Faulkner. When your essay appears as a solid mass to a grader who has but minutes to spend per paper, you can imagine the result.

Instead, make your essay easy on the eyes. Use paragraphs to show your progression of thought and the sequence of your analysis. Indent and skip a line between paragraphs. Whatever you do to make your grader's job easier, makes you the grateful beneficiary.

2. Do Not Overly Rely on Underlining, Capitalizing, Etc.

The effect is lost if you emphasize everything you write. You do not need to underline critical language because if you are writing in the language of the law, all you write is worthy of note. In fact, the better course of action is not to underline or write in all "caps" at all. Instead, use sub-headings and other organizational devices to guide the reader.

G. Emergency Measures or "What to Do if"

1. You Freeze and Begin to Panic

Aside from the usual exam jitters, the bar exam does present a unique set of circumstances. After all, it's not many tests that we take with hundreds or even thousands of other candidates at the same time and place. The surroundings alone prove problematic for some. Assuming, however, that this is not the cause of your fright but rather, you've just read the question and your mind has gone blank.

If you begin to feel panicky, stop whatever you are doing and breathe deeply. You want to regain your sense of control and composure immediately. Implement the following step-by-step approach:

- Quickly reread the question.

- Start with what you know: identify the area of law and see if it provides insight.

- Focus carefully on the facts, going paragraph by paragraph: what are they telling you? Ask why they are there. If you ask why, then you will find the answer. Except for some facts that are necessary to set up the story, practically every fact is there for a reason and the operative facts tend to be repeated more than once.

- Look to the "four-corners" of the MEE. What you are looking to find is contained within the four-corners of the document, not outside of it. This is your universe.

- Focus on the basics. See if you can provide definitions. Remember, rules are just definitions. The next step is to see if you can build on these definitions to write your paragraph of law.

- Summon the resources you developed in law school. Lawyers act; they do not react. Think deliberately and respond accordingly.

- If none of this works after a few minutes, and we mean no more than three minutes, then move on to the next MEE. When you've finished the others and return to this one, it's likely that you will see what you could not see before. The mind just works that way.

2. You Don't Know the Rule of Law

This is everyone's greatest fear, law student and lawyer alike. What you must do is learn to rely on your training and instinct. Force yourself to go through the following steps:

First, ask

"What is the issue?" You can formulate this from the question you are directed to answer. Even if you're not sure of the rule, you can identify the legal problem in the facts. Focusing on identifying the issue will allow you to regain your composure and lead you back to the structure of thinking like a lawyer.

Write the issue, whether or not you "know" the rule you need to apply. Formulating the issue will get you points from the grader because it shows that you can identify the legal problem from the facts.

Next, ask

"What principle of law is implicated by this issue?" Now you're thinking like a lawyer.

This will either lead you to the rule from the recesses of your memory or you'll have to improvise. When you improvise, rely on your knowledge of general legal principles and standards to guide you. Use what you know about the law in general to build a specific rule for your problem.

In such cases, begin by identifying the general legal concept implicated in the problem. Then move on to consider the following:

- Has there been a violation of a fiduciary obligation?

- Are the standards of due process /equal protection implicated?

- Has the requirement of good faith been breached?

- Are the "best interests of the child" at stake?

These questions become your starting point. As you study, you'll find more basic questions that you can rely on to trigger your thought process. Think of them as your mental checklist or playbook.

For example, if you're asked about recoverable damages in a particular case, rely on what you know about damages in particular areas of the law and proceed from there.

- If it's a contracts problem, you know that every breach of contract entitles the aggrieved party to sue for damages. The general theory of damages in contract actions is that the injured party should be placed in the same position as if the contract had been properly performed, at least so far as money can do this. Compensatory damages are designed to give the plaintiff the "benefit of his bargain."

- On the other hand, if it's a torts problem, you know that the overall goal is to compensate plaintiff for unreasonable harm which he or she has sustained.

And finally, even if you can't find the issue or principle of law, you can break down the problem into the elements common to every case and proceed from there:

- Identify the parties and the nature of their relationship.

Is it that of employer/employee, landlord/ tenant, buyer/seller, parent/child, husband/ wife?

- Identify the place(s) where the facts arose.

  Did the events occur in a public area, a private home, a school, a waterway, a farm?

- Identify whether objects or things were involved.

  Was there a transaction involving the sale of goods? Is the ownership of land or chattel in dispute?

- Identify the acts or omissions which form the basis of the action.

  Was there a robbery, an assault, an act of discrimination?

- Determine whether there is a defense to the action.

  Is there a basis for self-defense, justification, privilege?

- Characterize the relief sought.

  Are the parties seeking damages? Are they monetary or equitable damages, or both?

These questions allow you to gain access to the problem when your initial read is fruitless. From any one of these topics, it is but a short step to finding the principle of law implicated in the question. It might be a very good idea to memorize these topics and have them readily available to "jump-start" your thought process.

H. A Checklist for Writing "Bar-Right" MEEs

Have you followed the steps for writing point-worthy MEEs?

1. Do you know how much time to allocate for each question?

2. Have you "de-constructed" past MEEs to become familiar with:

   □ The difference between a "general" vs. a "specific" style essay?

   □ How different subject areas are combined within a single essay?

   □ How bar examiners use vocabulary to signal issues?

   □ How bar examiners use vocabulary to identify non-issues?

   □ Patterns in questions and the frequency of particular topics?

3. Have you "de-constructed the Analyses Sheets to see:

   □ How they follow the steps of a basic IRAC analysis?

   □ How to use the "whether, when" construction to state an issue that combines rule with operative facts?

   □ How to use "because", "since", "as and "when", to write a solid analysis that combines law and fact?

I. Automating the MEE Writing Process

Have you internalized the process of reading and answering MEEs so that it will be automatic for you on bar day?

Do you know to:

1. Allocate your time for each question and set up your clock on scrap paper?

2. Scan the six MEEs but return to the first to answer the questions in order while remaining flexible to answer out of sequence if you need to?

3. When you start to read, do you:

   ☐ Begin with the interrogatory at the end of the question?

   ☐ Identify whether it's a "specific" or "general"-style essay?

4. On reading the question for the first time, do you:

   ☐ Read through it to determine the subject area and get a sense of the problem and the parties, beginning with the call-of-the question?

   ☐ Reread the interrogatories and set up your outline on your laptop?

5. On your second reading, do you read actively to:

   ☐ Identify the area of law and the legal relationship of the parties?

   ☐ Circle amounts of money, dates, locations, quantities, ages, and words that express intent and knowledge?

   ☐ Note such key words as "oral" and "written"?

☐ Characterize legal issues in words with a question mark at the end so that you are not concluding but raising a question?

☐ Add to your outline as you proceed through each paragraph?

6. When writing the answer, do you follow an IRAC-based analysis and:

☐ Use the "whether, when" construction to combine rule and fact when writing the issue?

☐ Consider the rule in terms of context and consequences?

☐ Write a complete paragraph of law by compiling the building blocks for the rule of law by considering

the general rule?

exceptions to the general rule?

limitations to the rule?

defenses?

☐ Follow a hierarchy of concepts by

moving from the general to the specific?

defining each legal term of art?

☐ Introduce your analysis with *"Here"* or *"In this case"*?

☐ Match each "rule" with a "fact" using "because" to link the two?

☐ Conclude and continue to the next issue?

CHAPTER 4

Practice Makes Points

You don't get better at thinking about questions without practicing questions. Facts in a hypothetical "present" like symptoms in a patient. And like the doctor, you need to identify the problem from the presentation of the symptoms. It helps with the diagnosis if you've seen it before and not just read about it in a medical book.

We could have chosen almost any MEE to illustrate the strategies we've discussed because no matter what the subject, all the MEEs are constructed the same. Still, some MEEs are better than others for illustrative purposes because they are more obvious and thus easier for the novice to see. Once you know what to look for, you will see what you need to see in all MEEs, but it's best to begin with the clearest examples.

Please note that your bar exam questions will not come labeled by subject area. You will figure it out for yourself as you work through the problem. Still, do not be so concerned with labeling the subject into set categories because the questions may combine subjects. For learning purposes, we are identifying the MEE by exam administration and topic.

A. De-constructing a Typical MEE

Before we examine individual MEEs to illustrate specific strategies, it's helpful to consider a few questions and see what makes them representative of most MEEs. We've chosen a Torts question and two (2) Family Law questions.

What do we mean by a typical question? We mean "typical" in terms of the following:

- Subject area, e.g., assault, battery, negligence, consideration, jurisdiction

- Settings and sub-topics, e.g., "employer, employee," "eggshell skull," pre-existing conditions"

- Length (number of paragraphs) and structure of the question

- Number of issues

- Use of language

1. Torts: February 2010

This MEE is an excellent example of what you can expect to see on the bar exam for a Torts question, substantively, and for any question, structurally.

a. Substantively

This question assesses your knowledge of Tort law regarding battery and negligence. The main causes of action are identified for you, but you will have to identify the related issues of vicarious liability and liability for pre-existing conditions. It is amazing how many people in MEEville are afflicted with "eggshell skulls"!

b.   Structurally

- Number of paragraphs: there are five paragraphs for the story and one paragraph that sets out the claims. This last paragraph expands on the interrogatories. It is common on MEEs for the paragraph preceding the call-of-the question to identify the parties' causes of action, claims, or defenses. Read them carefully since they provide the theories of the case.

- Number of interrogatories: there are only two questions but it's important not to be deceived because every MEE has a minimum of three issues and usually four. As we discussed earlier, it depends on how you break down your analysis, but there are often sub-issues so be sure to use the numbered interrogatories as only a guide.

  Here, the sub-issues become clear when you re-read the paragraph where Penny outlines the claims she is bringing against Dennis: battery and negligence. Once you have these two claims, you can set up sub-headings under the first interrogatory.

  Further, once you take up the second question regarding the liability of the Fernbury Flies, your sub-issues increase from the basic negligence claim to include vicarious liability and the "eggshell" victim.

2.   *Reading the Question*

On the next pages, you will find the unmarked July 2010 MEE question and a marked-up version. The annotated version is an example of the MEE after it's been read "actively." We marked up the text with "X's and O's", numbered the paragraphs, and expressed our thoughts with question marks. It's probably a lot neater than it would be on exam day, but you get the idea.

As you can see, what you need to answer each question is contained in at most three short paragraphs. Careful reading of the facts is essential and easy to do when you mark the paragraphs.

3. *Outlining the Answer Using the Rule/Fact Chart*

After reading the question, the next step is outlining your answer. We've used the Rule/Chart to map out what a handwritten outline might look like. Once again, our chart is probably a lot neater than it would be on exam day but we had to be clear so you could read what we wrote.

On the exam, use your own form of shorthand to get to the point and note only the facts you need to connect with what you will write. Remember—the outline's objective is to guide your writing so make it as concise as possible—only what you need to prompt your thinking.

February 2010: Torts[1]

Penny lives in an apartment on Oak Street across from the Fernbury Baseball Park ("the Park"). The Park is owned and maintained by the Fernbury Flies, a professional minor league baseball team. As she left her apartment building one day, Penny was struck in the head by a baseball that had been hit by Dennis, a Flies player, during a game.

The section of Oak Street that adjoins the Park was once lined with single-family homes. Over the past two decades, these homes have been replaced by stores and apartment buildings, causing an increase in both car and pedestrian traffic on Oak Street.

The ball that struck Penny was one of the longest that had been hit at the Park since its construction 40 years ago. During the last 40 years, Flies' records show that only 30 balls had previously been hit over the Park fence adjoining Oak Street. Fifteen of the balls hit out of the Park onto Oak Street were hit during the past decade.

The Park is surrounded by a 10-foot-high fence, which was built during the Park's construction. All other ballparks owned by clubs in the Flies' league are surrounded by fences of similar type and identical height. These fences are typical of those used by other minor league teams in the United States. However, in Japan, where ballparks are often located in congested urban neighborhoods, netting is typically attached to ballpark fences. This netting permits balls to go over a fence but captures balls before they can strike a bystander or car.

After being struck by the ball, Penny was taken by ambulance to a hospital emergency room. After tests, the treating physician told Penny that she had suffered a concussion. The physician prescribed

---

[1] The Multistate Essay Examination ("MEE®") has been reprinted by permission from the NCBE®. Copyright© 2010 by the National Conference of Bar Examiners. All rights reserved.

pain medication for Penny. However, because of a preexisting condition, she had an adverse reaction to the medication and suffered neurological damage resulting in the loss of sensation in her extremities.

Penny has sued Dennis, the player who hit the baseball that struck her, for battery and negligence. Penny has also sued the Fernbury Flies. She seeks to recover damages for the concussion and the neurological damage resulting from the medication.

1.   Does Penny have a viable tort claim against Dennis? Explain.

2.   Does Penny have a viable tort claim against the Fernbury Flies? Explain.

Reading the Question

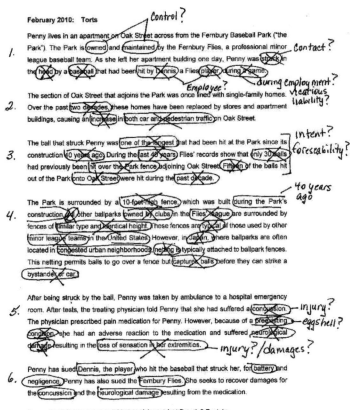

February 2010:   Torts   *Control?*

1. Penny lives in an apartment on Oak Street across from the Fernbury Baseball Park ("the Park"). The Park is owned and maintained by the Fernbury Flies, a professional minor   *Contact?* league baseball team. As she left her apartment building one day, Penny was struck in the head by a baseball that had been hit by Dennis, a Flies player, during a game.

Employee?   *during employment?*   *vicarious liability?*

2. The section of Oak Street that adjoins the Park was once lined with single-family homes. Over the past two decades, these homes have been replaced by stores and apartment buildings, causing an increase in both car and pedestrian traffic on Oak Street.

intent?   *foreseeability?*

3. The ball that struck Penny was one of the longest that had been hit at the Park since its construction 40 years ago. During the last 40 years, Flies' records show that only 30 balls had previously been hit over the Park fence adjoining Oak Street. Fifteen of the balls hit out of the Park onto Oak Street were hit during the past decade.

40 years ago

4. The Park is surrounded by a 10-foot-high fence, which was built during the Park's construction. All other ballparks owned by clubs in the Flies League are surrounded by fences of similar type and identical height. These fences are typical of those used by other minor league teams in the United States. However, in Japan, where ballparks are often located in congested urban neighborhoods, netting is typically attached to ballpark fences. This netting permits balls to go over a fence but captures balls before they can strike a bystander or car.

5. After being struck by the ball, Penny was taken by ambulance to a hospital emergency room. After tests, the treating physician told Penny that she had suffered a concussion. *injury?* The physician prescribed pain medication for Penny. However, because of a preexisting *eggshell?* condition, she had an adverse reaction to the medication and suffered neurological damage resulting in the loss of sensation in her extremities. *injury? / damages?*

6. Penny has sued Dennis, the player who hit the baseball that struck her, for battery and negligence. Penny has also sued the Fernbury Flies. She seeks to recover damages for the concussion and the neurological damage resulting from the medication.

1.   Does Penny have a viable tort claim against Dennis? Explain.

2.   Does Penny have a viable tort claim against the Fernbury Flies? Explain.

Outlining the Answer Using the Rule/Fact Chart

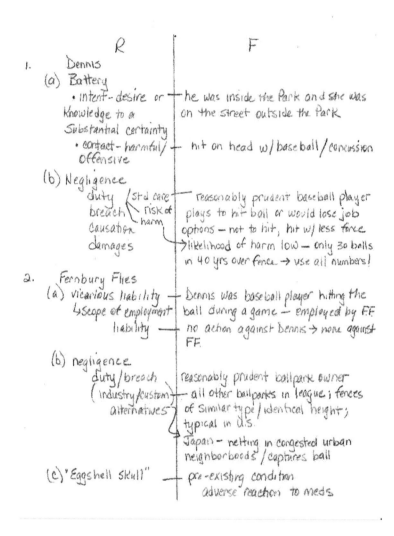

R | F

1. Dennis
   (a) Battery
   • Intent – desire or — he was inside the Park and she was
   knowledge to a   on the street outside the Park
   Substantial certainty
   • contact – harmful / — hit on head w/ baseball / concussion
   offensive

   (b) Negligence
   duty ⎰std care — reasonably prudent baseball player
   breach ⎱ risk of   plays to hit ball or would lose job
   Causation ⎵ harm   options – not to hit, hit w/ less force
   damages   →likelihood of harm low — only 30 balls
                      in 40 yrs over fence → use all numbers!

2. Fernbury Flies
   (a) vicarious liability — Dennis was baseball player hitting the
   ↳Scope of employment   ball during a game — employed by FF
   liability —— no action against Dennis → none against
                 FF.

   (b) negligence
   duty/breach   reasonably prudent ballpark owner
   (industry/custom)— all other ballparks in league; fences
   alternatives   of similar type / identical height;
                    typical in U.S.
                  Japan – netting in congested urban
                  neighborhoods / captures ball

   (c) "Eggshell Skull" — pre-existing condition
                          adverse reaction to meds

4. Family Law: July 2008, February 2018

We've included these two MEEs in Family Law to show the consistency of the questions. While a decade apart in time, these two MEEs are very similar in substance and language.

a. Substance

Both MEEs test the same issues and sub-issues: enforceability of a pre-marital agreement when given shortly before the wedding to the unsuspecting spouse; disclosure of assets and liabilities; questionable provisions in the pre-marital agreement; identification of the parties' separate and marital property; and, a reference to the Uniform Premarital Agreement Act.

b. Language

The words speak for themselves:

From July 2008:

- "Two weeks before their wedding Hal told Wendy that his lawyer (Lawyer) had advised him not to marry Wendy unless she signed a premarital agreement."

And from February 2018:

- "One week before their wedding, David surprised Meg by asking her to sign a premarital agreement prepared by his attorney" and "David told Meg that he would not proceed with the marriage unless she signed the agreement."

From July 2008:

- "Lawyer gave Wendy an accurate list of Hal's assets and a copy of Hal's tax returns for the past three years."

And from February 2018:

- "Attached to the proposed agreement was an accurate list of David's net assets (his personal possessions, the auto repair business, a used car, and a small bank account), a list of his liabilities, and his tax returns for the past three years."

July 2008: Family Law[2]

Six years ago, Hal and Wendy were married in State A. Both of them had been previously divorced. Hal, age 40, was a successful businessman earning $200,000 per year. Wendy, age 30, was a struggling songwriter earning $20,000 per year.

Two weeks before their wedding, Hal told Wendy that his lawyer (Lawyer) had advised him not to marry Wendy unless she signed a premarital agreement. Hal gave Wendy a copy of the agreement Lawyer had proposed and suggested that she review it with Lawyer or another attorney of her own choosing. The agreement specified that in the event of divorce:

1. Each spouse waives all claims to property acquired by the other during the first five years of the marriage;

2. The spouses will share joint physical and legal custody of any children born to them during the marriage.

When Hal gave Wendy the proposed agreement, she burst into tears. Wendy was very angry and hurt, but she did not want to call off the wedding at such a late date. Reluctantly, she agreed to discuss the matter with Lawyer.

Lawyer gave Wendy an accurate list of Hal's assets and a copy of Hal's tax returns for the past three years. Lawyer urged her to consult another attorney. After conferring with her family, but not an attorney, Wendy decided to sign the proposed agreement. The day before their wedding, she and Hal signed the agreement in Lawyer's office in State A.

---

[2]   The Multistate Essay Examination ("MEE®") has been reprinted by permission from the NCBE®. Copyright© 2008 by the National Conference of Bar Examiners. All rights reserved.

Four years ago, Hal and Wendy had a child (Child).

Six months ago, Hal and Wendy moved to State B. Hal's business has continued to prosper. He currently earns $300,000 per year. Since the marriage, Hal has used his business income to acquire assets worth about $500,000. Wendy has continued to write songs. Her current income is $30,000 per year.

Three months ago, after Wendy discovered that Hal was having an affair, she took Child and moved back to State A, where she plans to remain. Since leaving Hal, Wendy has written and recorded several songs about her marriage. Wendy's agent believes that these songs "will hit the top of the charts."

State A has adopted the Uniform Premarital Agreement Act. State B has not. The premarital agreement contains no choice-of-law provision.

1. Which state's law governs the enforceability of the premarital agreement? Explain.

2. Is the waiver-of-property-rights provision in the premarital agreement enforceable? Explain.

3. Is the child-custody provision in the premarital agreement enforceable? Explain.

4. Are the profits to be derived from Wendy's songs written after she left Hal subject to division at divorce? Explain.

February 2018: Family Law[3]

In 2012, David and Meg had a baby girl, Anna. At the time of Anna's birth, David and Meg were both 21 years old. For the next four years, they lived separately. David and Anna lived with David's mother (Anna's grandmother). The grandmother cared for Anna while David worked. David cared for Anna most evenings and weekends. During this period, Meg attended college in a distant city; she called weekly but visited Anna only during school breaks and for one month each summer.

In 2013, David bought an auto repair business with money he had saved. The grandmother continued to care for Anna while David was working in his auto repair business.

In 2016, David and Meg were married in a small wedding held at the grandmother's house. One week before their wedding, David surprised Meg by asking her to sign a premarital agreement prepared by his attorney. The agreement provided that, in the event of a divorce,

1. all assets owned by each spouse at the time of the marriage would remain the sole property of that spouse;

2. neither spouse would be entitled to alimony; and

3. the spouses would have joint physical custody of Anna.

Attached to the proposed agreement was an accurate list of David's net assets (his personal possessions, the auto repair business, a used car, and a small bank account), a list of his liabilities, and his tax returns for the past three years.

David told Meg that he would not proceed with the marriage unless she signed the agreement. Meg believed that the marriage would be successful, and she did not want to cancel or postpone the wedding. She therefore signed the agreement and appended a list of her own debts (student loans); she correctly indicated that she had no assets other than her personal possessions.

Since the wedding, David, Meg, and Anna have lived together and the grandmother has continued to provide child care while David and Meg are at work. Meg has worked full-time as a computer engineer, and David has continued to work full-time in his auto repair business. Their incomes are relatively equal.

They have the following assets: (a) the auto repair business (owned by David); (b) stocks (owned by Meg, which she inherited last year); and (c) the marital home (purchased by David in his name alone shortly after the wedding). The down payment and all mortgage payments for the marital home have come from the couple's employment income.

Last month, David discovered that Meg had been having an affair with a coworker for the past year.

David wants a divorce. He also wants to obtain sole physical custody of Anna; he believes that Meg's adultery should disqualify her as a custodial parent. His plan is to live with the grandmother, who would provide child care when he is unavailable.

This jurisdiction has adopted a statute modeled after the Uniform Premarital Agreement Act.

1. May either spouse successfully enforce the premarital agreement in whole or in part? Explain.

2. Assuming that the premarital agreement is not enforceable, what assets are divisible at divorce? Explain.

3. Assuming that the premarital agreement is not enforceable, may David obtain sole physical custody of Anna based on (a) Meg's adultery or (b) other factors? Explain.

B. Getting Organized: "Follow the Yellow Brick Road"

"Follow the Yellow Brick Road" to write a well-organized answer by using the question's numbering scheme.

1. Outlining with Numbered Interrogatories: July 2016

We selected the Corporations and LLC question from the July 2016 bar administration because the interrogatories provide a clear writing path and all you have to do is follow them.

This MEE is also an excellent example of how to recognize the "clues" in the bar examiners' specific use of language to lead you to the issue and the rule.

a. MEE Chart

We charted the question to show how the paragraphs match up with the interrogatories. We also numbered each paragraph. When you look at an MEE this way, it is easy to see how tightly it is constructed where each issue is tied to only one or two paragraphs. This structure allows you to focus intently on one issue at a time. We suggest that you get in the habit of numbering the paragraphs as you read them.

b. MEE Outline

We followed the steps in Chapter 3, section D, subsection 5, Outline Your Answer, to create a working outline. While our outline is a lot more formal that the one you would create on exam day, it's still a good example of how you set up your outline as you work your way through the question.

Although the outline appears in its entirety, it was not written that way; rather it was written in the following sequence as noted above in Chapter 3:

1. Numbers: Set up the outline structure by writing the numbers from the interrogatories

2. Issues: Went back to the first question and identified the issue using the "whether, when"

3. Rules: Bulleted the applicable rules for that issue

4. Facts: Went back to the paragraphs for that issue and identified the relevant facts based on the rules

Repeated the process of Issue, Rules, and Facts for each issue.

c. Clues in the Language

Although it might not seem as if the bar examiners are trying to help you, it's hard to find another reason for the number of clues and prompts provided in the questions. This assistance comes in two forms: first, by using the language of the law in presenting the story; and, second, by making statements that just beg you to respond.

Let's identify the leading words and phrases by paragraph:

Paragraph 1: Certificate of organization to form a limited liability company

Brother and sister paid for their LLC member interests by each contributing $100,000 in cash to the LLC

Cousin paid . . .by conveying to the LLC. . .farmland valued at $100,000

Paragraph 2: Neither certificate of organization nor member's operating agreement specifies whether the LLC is member-managed or manager-managed *(prompt to ask: what happens when silent?)*

Operating agreement provides LLC's farmland may not be sold without the approval of all three members

Paragraph 4: Purporting to act on behalf of the LLC

Twice before he had purchased tires for the LLC at the same price from this manufacturer and neither his sister nor their cousin had objected

The tires "are perfect for the bikes we sell"

"You bought them without my permission" *(Prompt to ask: does he need her permission to buy tires for the bike store?)*

"I didn't need your permission" *(Prompt to ask: in case you missed it when the sister said he needed her permission)*

Paragraph 5: Purporting to act on behalf of the LLC

Cousin sold LLC's farmland to third-party buyer

Paid $120,000, which was well above the land's fair market value *(Prompt to ask: does it matter that the sale made a profit for the LLC?)*

Learned of the sale only after the sale proceeds were deposited

Both of them objected

Paragraph 6: Wrote in an email

"I want out of our business"

Send me a check "for my share" *(Prompt to ask: what if anything is the brother entitled to receive?*

July 2016: Corporations and Limited Liability Companies[4]

Two siblings, a brother and a sister, decided to start a bike shop with their cousin. They filed a certificate of organization to form a limited liability company. The brother and the sister paid for their LLC member interests by each contributing $100,000 in cash to the LLC. Their cousin paid for his LLC member interest by conveying to the LLC five acres of farmland valued at $100,000; the LLC then recorded the deed.

Neither the certificate of organization nor the members' operating agreement specifies whether the LLC is member-managed or manager-managed. However, the operating agreement provides that the LLC's farmland may not be sold without the approval of all three members.

Following formation of the LLC, the company rented a storefront commercial space for the bike shop and opened for business.

Three months ago, purporting to act on behalf of the LLC, the brother entered into a written and signed contract to purchase 100 bike tires for $6,000 from a tire manufacturer. When the tires were delivered, the sister said that they were too expensive and told her brother to return the tires. The brother was surprised by his sister's objection because twice before he had purchased tires for the LLC at the same price from this manufacturer, and neither his sister nor their cousin had objected. The brother refused to return the tires, pointing out that the tires "are perfect for the bikes we sell." The sister responded, "Well, pay the bill with your own money; you bought them without my permission." The brother responded, "No way. I bought these for the store, I didn't need

---

your permission, and the company will pay for them." To date, however, the $6,000 has not been paid.

One month ago, purporting to act on behalf of the LLC, the cousin sold the LLC's farmland to a third-party buyer. The buyer paid $120,000, which was well above the land's fair market value. Only after the cousin deposited the sale proceeds into the LLC bank account did the brother and sister learn of the sale. Both of them objected.

One week ago, the brother wrote in an email to his sister, "I want out of our business. I don't want to have anything to do with the bike shop anymore. Please send me a check for my share."

1. What type of LLC was created—member-managed or manager-managed? Explain.

2. Is the LLC bound under the tire contract? Explain.

3. Is the LLC bound by the sale of the farmland? Explain.

4. What is the legal effect of the brother's email? Explain.

July 2016: Corporations and Limited Liability Companies

By the Paragraph	Fact Pattern
¶ 1 Question 1: covered in paragraphs 1&2	Two siblings, a brother and a sister, decided to start a bike shop with their cousin. They filed a certificate of organization to form a limited liability company. The brother and the sister paid for their LLC member interests by each contributing $100,000 in cash to the LLC. Their cousin paid for his LLC member interest by conveying to the LLC five acres of farmland valued at $100,000; the LLC then recorded the deed.
¶ 2	Neither the certificate of organization nor the members' operating agreement specifies whether the LLC is member-managed or manager-managed. However, the operating agreement provides that the LLC's farmland may not be sold without the approval of all three members.
¶ 3 Question 2: covered in paragraphs 3&4	Following formation of the LLC, the company rented a storefront commercial space for the bike shop and opened for business.
¶ 4	Three months ago, purporting to act on behalf of the LLC, the brother entered into a written and signed contract to purchase 100 bike tires for $6,000 from a tire manufacturer. When the tires were delivered, the sister said that they were

	too expensive and told her brother to return the tires. The brother was surprised by his sister's objection because twice before he had purchased tires for the LLC at the same price from this manufacturer, and neither his sister nor their cousin had objected. The brother refused to return the tires, pointing out that the tires "are perfect for the bikes we sell." The sister responded, "Well, pay the bill with your own money; you bought them without my permission." The brother responded, "No way. I bought these for the store, I didn't need your permission, and the company will pay for them." To date, however, the $6,000 has not been paid.
¶ 5 Question 3: covered in paragraph 5	One month ago, purporting to act on behalf of the LLC, the cousin sold the LLC's farmland to a third-party buyer. The buyer paid $120,000, which was well above the land's fair market value. Only after the cousin deposited the sale proceeds into the LLC bank account did the brother and sister learn of the sale. Both of them objected.
¶ 6 Question 4: covered in paragraph 6	One week ago, the brother wrote in an email to his sister, "I want out of our business. I don't want to have anything to do with the bike shop anymore. Please send me a check for my share."
	1. What type of LLC was created—member-managed or manager—managed? Explain.

	2. Is the LLC bound under the tire contract? Explain.
	3. Is the LLC bound by the sale of the farmland? Explain.
	4. What is the legal effect of the brother's email? Explain.

Outline for July 2016 MEE

1. The issue is whether the LLC is member-managed or manager-managed when the certificate of organization and the members' operating agreement is silent.

Rules

- Default applies when the certification of organization and operating agreement are silent.

- Presumption is member-managed.

Facts

- Cert of org and operating agreement are silent so default rule applies.

2. The issue is whether the brother had authority to purchase the tires so as to bind the LLC when he had purchased tires for the LLC at the same prices from this manufacturer before without objection from the other members.

Rules

- Each member in a member-managed LLC has an equal say in the management and control of the company's activities.

- Each member can bind the company to contracts for apparently carrying on the ordinary business of the company unless the member lacks authority and the other party to the contracts knows that the member lacks authority.

Facts

- The brother was a member of the LLC—paid for his interest by contributing $100,000 in cash

- Purchased 100 bike tires from a tire manufacturer for the store

- The business of the company was a bike shop

- The brother had purchased tires for LLC twice before at same price from same manufacturer without objection from sister or cousin

- The tires "are perfect for the bikes we sell"

3. The issue is whether the cousin's sale on behalf of the LLC of the LLC's farmland binds the LLC when it was done without the approval of the other members as required in their operating agreement.

    Rules

    - Actual and apparent authority

    - Ordinary course of the LLC's business

    Facts

    - Operating agreement requires consent of all members to sell the farmland

    - The cousin sold the farmland without getting approval

    - Third-party buyer paid $120,000 which was well above the land's fair market value and $20,000 over its value at the time cousin conveyed to the LLC

4. The issue is whether the brother's withdrawal from the LLC caused a dissociation when he wrote that he wanted "out of our business."

    Rules

    - Dissociation vs dissolution

- Consequences of dissociation, including whether he has right to payment for LLC interest.

Facts

- The brother's email showed an express will to withdraw

- The brother requested a check for his share

2. Outlining with Hidden Interrogatories: July 2016

We selected the Civil Procedure question from the July 2016 bar administration to show how to outline your answer when numbered interrogatories are absent.

You will find a lot of MEEs structured like this one: while the usual numbered interrogatories are absent, you are given the party's three bases for dismissal instead. Consequently, you can set up your outline for this MEE as follows:

(a) Lack of personal jurisdiction

(b) Lack of subject-matter jurisdiction

(c) Improper venue

Each basis for dismissal provides the basis for your issue statement. Once you have your issues, follow the usual steps for the rules and the facts.

July 2016: Civil Procedure[5]

A woman and a man have both lived their entire lives in State A. The man once went to a gun show in State B where he bought a gun. Otherwise, neither the woman nor the man had ever left State A until the following events occurred.

The woman and the man went hunting for wild turkey at a State A game preserve. The man was carrying the gun he had purchased in State B. The man had permanently disabled the gun's safety features to be able to react more quickly to a turkey sighting. The man dropped the gun and it accidentally fired, inflicting a serious chest wound on the woman. The woman was immediately flown to a hospital in neighboring State C, where she underwent surgery.

One week after the shooting accident, the man traveled to State C for business and took the opportunity to visit the woman in the hospital. During the visit, the woman's attorney handed the man the summons and complaint in a suit the woman had initiated against the man in the United States District Court for the District of State C. Two days later, the woman was released from the hospital and returned home to State A where she spent weeks recovering.

The woman's complaint alleges separate claims against the man: 1) a state-law negligence claim and 2) a federal claim under the Federal Gun Safety Act (Safety Act). The Safety Act provides a cause of action for individuals harmed by gun owners who alter the safety features of a gun that has traveled in interstate commerce. The Safety Act caps damages at $100,000 per incident, but does not preempt state causes of action. The woman's complaint seeks damages of $100,000 on the Safety Act claim and $120,000 on the

---

[5]   The Multistate Essay Examination ("MEE®") has been reprinted by permission from the NCBE®. Copyright© 2016 by the National Conference of Bar Examiners. All rights reserved.

state-law negligence claim. Both sets of damages are sought as compensation for the physical suffering the woman experienced and the medical costs the woman incurred as a result of the shooting.

The man has moved to dismiss the complaint, asserting (a) lack of personal jurisdiction, (b) lack of subject-matter jurisdiction, and (c) improper venue. State C's jurisdictional statutes provide that state courts may exercise personal jurisdiction "to the limits allowed by the United States Constitution."

With respect to each asserted basis for dismissal, should the man's motion to dismiss be granted? Explain.

3. Outlining Without Interrogatories: February 2012

We selected the Corporations question from the February 2012 bar administration as an example to show how to develop your outline when there are no interrogatories but only a general question followed by "Explain."

This type of question is a bit more challenging to outline, but only a bit. Following the procedures outlined in Chapter 3 for working with a general-style essay, the first step is to number the paragraphs. Then proceed paragraph by paragraph, identifying and numbering the issues as you find them.

If you proceed in this manner, it's likely that you will identify the following issues:

1. Whether the directors received proper notice of the special meeting when it was sent by overnight mail 30 days before the meeting was to be held.

2. Whether Claire received proper notice of the special meeting when notice was not sent to her because the

corporation did not have a current mailing address for her.

3. Whether Claire waived notice of the meeting when she attended the meeting on March 31.

4. Whether there was a quorum present at the special meeting of the board of directors.

5. Whether the purchase of the asset received a majority vote of the directors when two directors called in by phone and could not hear each other.

Once you have the issues, follow the usual steps for the rules and the facts. When you've completed your outline, you may need to review the sequence of issues into a logical order for your written analysis.

February 2012: Corporations[6]

A corporation's articles of incorporation state that the corporation shall have a seven-member board of directors. Neither the articles of incorporation nor the corporation's bylaws contain any special provisions regarding the board of directors.

On March 1, the corporation's president told its secretary to convene a special meeting of the board of directors. Accordingly, the secretary prepared a Notice of Special Meeting (Notice) and sent it by overnight mail to six of the seven directors. The secretary did not send the Notice to the seventh director—Claire—because Claire had recently moved and the corporation did not have a current mailing address for her.

The Notice stated only that a special meeting of the corporation's board of directors would be held on March 31 at 10 a.m., at the corporate headquarters.

On March 2, each member of the board of directors except Claire received the Notice. Directors Alan and Barb, both of whom had vacation plans for March 31, made arrangements with the secretary to participate in the special meeting by telephone.

On March 30, Alan called Claire and informed her that a special meeting of the board of directors was going to be held on March 31.

On March 31, five members of the board of directors (including Claire but neither Alan nor Barb) gathered in the corporation's conference room. Alan and Barb called in from their vacation homes. The five directors present in the conference room could hear both Alan and Barb. Alan and Barb could each hear the five directors in the conference room but could not hear each other.

---

[6] The Multistate Essay Examination ("MEE®") has been reprinted by permission from the NCBE®. Copyright© 2012 by the National Conference of Bar Examiners. All rights reserved.

After a lengthy discussion, the board of directors voted 4-3 to approve the corporation's purchase of a major asset. Alan and Barb both voted to approve the purchase.

Claire, who voted against the purchase, is very upset and has brought an action seeking an injunction to prevent the purchase of the asset. Claire asserts that the board of directors did not properly approve the purchase of the asset.

Did the board of directors properly approve the purchase of the asset? Explain.

C. Using the Clues in the "4-Corners of the MEE"

You can use the "clues" in the bar examiners' specific use of language to lead you to the issue and the rule. Often, the clues are written in the language of the rule itself. This is not an accident: the bar examiners are providing prompts to direct you where you need to go. The careful reader will not ignore these gifts but look for them actively and use them to facilitate memory and recall.

1. Hiding in Plain Sight

We chose the Agency question from the February 2017 bar administration to show how the language in the question can prompt your memory to retrieve the relevant rule. We've italicized and highlighted the relevant language in the MEE that follows but it's pretty hard to miss the agency issues when the word "agent" is used five (5) times!

But this is not the only clue—if one can even call it a clue. Consider this sentence: "She told the manufacturer that she was the *inventor's agent* and that she wanted to purchase 25 Series A computer chips *on his behalf.*" Not only are the bar examiners telling you that she was an agent, but they are giving you its definition. All you have to do to write the rule is to put the pieces together: an agent is one who acts on behalf of another, "the principal."

Suppose, however, that you could not remember that the other party in the agency relationship is the principal. All you had to do was read the last paragraph before the interrogatories: *"When she signed the contract, she told the manufacturer that she was acting as someone's agent but did not disclose the identity of her principal."* Not only does this sentence provide the key word, "principal," but it signals the issue regarding disclosure of the principal's identity. There are several prompts in the narrative where the woman is either disclosing or not disclosing to the manufacturers the identity of the principal. These references should remind you to consider the significance of disclosed vs. undisclosed principals.

2. Using the Rule/Fact Chart

We also like this question to show how to use the Rule/Fact chart to outline your answer and guide your thinking. We've stated the issue and outlined the rules and facts for the first interrogatory. While our chart looks very formal because we've prepared it for a book, your chart should be much simpler. It's just meant to assist you in lining up the relevant facts and law. Don't make it complicated. Use your own shorthand to identify the rules but do not skimp on the facts. Note the specificity with which we identified the facts—you must do the same to ensure that they appear in your analysis.

February 2017: Agency[7]

An inventor retained a woman *to act as his agent* to purchase 25 computer chips, 25 blue lenses, and 25 lawn mower shutoff switches. The *inventor told her to purchase only*:

- Series A computer chips,

- blue lenses that cost no more than $300 each, and

- shutoff switches that could shut down a lawn mower in less than one second after the mower hits a foreign object.

The woman contacted a chip manufacturer to purchase the Series A computer chips. She told the manufacturer that she was the *inventor's agent* and that she wanted to purchase 25 Series A computer chips *on his behalf*. The manufacturer told her that the Series A chips cost $800 each but that she could buy Series B chips, with functionality similar to that of the Series A chips, for only $90 each. Without discussing this with the inventor, the woman agreed to purchase 25 Series B chips, signing the contract with the chip manufacturer *"as agent" of the inventor*. The Series B chips were shipped to her, but when she then took them to the inventor and explained what a great deal she had gotten, the inventor refused to accept them. He has also refused to pay the manufacturer for them.

The woman also contacted a lens manufacturer for the purchase of the blue lenses. She signed a contract in her name alone for the purchase of 25 blue lenses at $295 per lens. She did not tell the lens manufacturer that she was acting as anyone's *agent*. The lenses were shipped to her, but when she took them to the inventor, he refused to accept them because he had decided that it would be

---

better to use red lenses. The inventor has refused to pay for the blue lenses.

The woman also contacted a switch manufacturer to purchase shutoff switches. She signed a contract in her name alone for switches that would shut down a lawn mower in less than five seconds, a substantially slower reaction time than the inventor had specified to her. When she signed the contract, she told the manufacturer that she was acting as someone's *agent* but did not disclose the identity of her *principal*. The switches were shipped to her. Although the inventor recognized that the switches were not what the woman had been told to buy, he nonetheless used them to build lawn mowers, but now refuses to pay the manufacturer for them.

All elements of contract formation and enforceability are satisfied with respect to each contract.

(1) Who is liable to the chip manufacturer: the inventor, the woman, or both? Explain.

(2) Who is liable to the blue-lens manufacturer: the inventor, the woman, or both? Explain.

(3) Who is liable to the shutoff-switch manufacturer: the inventor, the woman, or both? Explain.

Rule/Fact Chart for Issue 1

Issue: Whether the woman was liable for the contract when she was told to purchase Series B chips but instead purchased Series A.

Rule(s)	Fact(s)
UCC/sale of goods but UCC does not have agency rules so supplement with CL	Sale of computer chips
Agent: one who acts on behalf of another, the principal; disclosed principal	Woman told by inventor to purchase 25 computer chips for him
Actual authority; exceeding scope of authority	Told to purchase **only** Series A; Purchased Series B w/out discussing w/inventor
Apparent authority; implied warranty of authority to third party	Told manufacturer she was inventor's agent Signed contract "as agent" of inventor Chips were shipped to her Inventor refused to accept and pay.

D. "X's and O's"

We selected the Contracts question from the February 2018 bar administration to show the use of "X's and O's" in writing a solid analysis. First, however, we thought that we'd review and summarize the steps for active reading that we covered in Chapter 3, section D, subsection 4 so that they would be fresh in your mind:

1.   Identify the area of law and the legal relationship between the parties: employer and employee, husband and wife, buyer and seller, landlord and tenant, etc., by writing the words.

2.   Circle amounts of money, dates, locations, quantities, ages, words that go to "knowledge" and "intent", "public" and "private", "oral" and "written" and the numerous variations that lead to the same result: he "phoned", he "called", "she sent an email", "she sent a fax."

3.   Circle the words in a bubble, like a big "O." This ensures that relevant facts pop out of the text so you don't miss them. When writing the analysis, you will go back and check the facts, "X'ing" out each "O" as you incorporate that fact into your discussion.

4   Identify issues by stating them and with a question mark: "merchants?", "excited utterance?", "anticipatory repudiation?", "breach?"

We've placed the relevant language in bold to identify what should be "O's" and then crossed them out to show them as "X's" after they have been "used" in writing the analysis. It is so much simpler to do this with pencil and paper but you can get the idea this way as well. While your mark-up of the text would include the comments that we mention in steps 1 and 3, we omitted them in this context because our focus was solely on the types of words and phrases that get circled. We've also limited what's "X'd" or crossed out to the facts and phrases relevant to the two issues we take up with the Fact Whisperer in section E below.

E. "The Fact Whisperer"

The Contracts question from the February 2018 is also an excellent example for showing how the Fact Whisperer comes into play. It works in two ways:

1. *Letting the Facts Lead You to the Legal Problem*

When you don't see the issue at first, you can let the facts lead you to the legal problem. Here is where you ask, "Why is this fact here?" There must be a reason. Aside from a few facts that may be needed to provide context and setting, the facts in the problem are there for a purpose, especially any dialogue between the parties. Let's look at some examples.

a. **The Modification Issue**

Consider, for example, these statements regarding the price change for the woman to serve as the potter's apprentice:

". . .the potter said that he had *decided* that the $4,000 price was too high for the right to serve as his apprentice and *proposed lowering* it to $3,500. The woman happily *agreed*, and they shook hands on this *new arrangement*."

together with,

". . .the potter pointed to the *Memorandum of Agreement* and said to the woman, 'That's *not what this says. This says that you'll pay me $4,000* today. *Even if I agreed to lower the price, I didn't get anything for that, so why should I be bound by it*'?"

Assuming that you did not know what to make of this conversation when you first read it, you would go back and let the facts speak to you:

- The parties had an *existing agreement* for the woman to pay the potter $4,000.

- Subsequently, the potter *decided* the price was too high and *proposed lowering* it to $3,500.

- The woman *agreed*; they shook hands on this *new arrangement.*

At this point, you should see that the parties orally agreed to change an existing agreement. Now add in the following facts:

- The original agreement was in writing in the *Memorandum of Agreement.*

- The writing says **$4,000** and the subsequent oral agreement is for **$3,500.**

- Even if the potter *agreed, "I didn't get anything for that, so why should I be bound by it'*?"

At this point, the issue should be clear since the potter is practically spelling it out for you: whether the parties' modification is enforceable when one party gives up the right to $500 and gets nothing in exchange.

The facts are intended to lead you to the consideration issue: how else could you read, "I didn't get anything for that so why should I be bound by it?"

b. The Lodging Issue

We can follow the same process with the lodging question and the facts will, once again, lead us to issue.

- The potter . . . *said that their deal did not require him to provide lodging for the woman.*

- When the *woman protested that they had agreed to the lodging arrangement*, the potter took *the signed Memorandum of Agreement* . . . and pointed out . . . that it contained *no reference to the woman's living in his studio*. He then said, *"If it's not in here, it's not part of the deal."*

The facts are setting up the question whether the potter is bound to provide lodging when it was part of the parties' oral agreement but not contained in their subsequent written Memorandum of Agreement. The clues all lead to the parol evidence rule.

2. *Ensuring That You Write a Complete Analysis*

When you match up the requirements of the rule with the facts, you explain why the rule is applicable. Explaining where each relevant fact belongs is like putting the pieces of the puzzle together to complete the picture.

Contracts: February 2018[8]

A woman whose hobby was making pottery wanted to improve her pottery skills both for her own enjoyment and to enable her to create some pottery items that she could sell. Accordingly, she entered into **negotiations** with an **experienced professional** potter about the possibility of an apprenticeship at his pottery studio.

The negotiations went well, and after some discussion, the woman and the professional potter ~~orally agreed~~ to the following on **May 1**:

- The woman would be the potter's apprentice for **three months** beginning **May 15**. During the apprenticeship, the potter would **provide education and guidance** about the artistry and business of pottery. The woman would pay the potter ~~$4,000~~ for the right to serve as the potter's apprentice, **payable on the first day** of the apprenticeship.

- The potter would **supply** the woman with **equipment and tools** that she would **use during the apprenticeship** and would be entitled to **take with her at the conclusion of the apprenticeship. On or before May 8**, the woman would pay the potter ~~$5,000 for the equipment and tools~~.

- The woman would be ~~provided with a private room in the potter's studio~~ in which to stay during the apprenticeship.

On **May 2**, the woman and the potter ~~signed~~ a document titled ~~"Memorandum of Agreement."~~ It ~~contained the terms orally agreed~~ to the day before, except that it ~~did not refer to the~~

~~woman's living in a private room in the potter's studio~~. The last sentence of the document stated, **"This is our complete agreement."**

On **May 8**, the woman went to the potter's studio and **paid him the $5,000** called for in the agreement for the equipment and tools. While she was there, the potter **said** that he had ~~decided~~ that the ~~$4,000 price was too high~~ for the right to serve as his apprentice and ~~proposed lowering it to $3,500~~. The **woman** happily ~~agreed~~, and they shook hands on this ~~new arrangement~~.

On **May 15**, the woman arrived at the potter's studio to begin the apprenticeship and move into the room she would occupy during that time. The potter refused to let her move in, however, and ~~said that their deal did not require him to provide lodging~~ for the woman. When the ~~woman protested that they had agreed to the lodging arrangement~~, the potter took the ~~signed Memorandum of Agreement~~ out of his pocket and pointed out to her that it contained ~~no reference to the woman's living in his studio~~. He then said, ~~"If it's not in here, it's not part of the deal."~~

The woman then said, "At least you were ~~reasonable in agreeing to change the price~~ for the apprenticeship to ~~$3,500~~. Saving that extra five hundred dollars means a lot to me." In response, the potter pointed to the ~~Memorandum of Agreement again~~ and said to the woman, ~~"That's not what this says. This says that you'll pay me $4,000 today. Even if I agreed to lower the price, I didn't get anything for that, so why should I be bound by it?"~~

The woman is quite angry about this turn of events and is considering suing the potter.

1. If the woman sues the potter about the disputes relating to the apprenticeship, will those disputes be governed by the common law of contracts or by Article 2 of the Uniform Commercial Code? Explain.

2. Assuming that the common law of contracts governs, is the oral agreement concerning the woman's lodging binding on the parties? Explain.

3. Assuming that the common law of contracts governs, is the oral agreement lowering the price for the apprenticeship binding on the parties? Explain.

CHAPTER 5

An MEE Make-Over
Using Legal Forensics

A. How Forensic IRAC Works with the MEE

As we discussed, an effective essay follows the IRAC structure. As a result, your essays should be organized around an "issue," a "rule," an "application," and a "conclusion" for each and every issue and sub-issue you identify on an exam question. Once you've written an essay, therefore, you have all the evidence you need to use our forensic principles. By examining what you've written through the legal lens of IRAC, you'll be able to evaluate your own work.

Forensic IRAC works by examining each sentence you've written in terms of its place in the IRAC structure of legal analysis. We've called the process forensic IRAC because the techniques we're going to use are similar to those employed by crime scene investigators, accountants, medical examiners, and any of the forensic experts who go back over the trail of evidence to determine how that evidence led to a particular result. While such experts rely on fingerprints, ballistics, ledger books, and DNA, we use IRAC.

We need to step inside your head to see the way you thought about the exam question—how you approached it, how you read the facts, and what they meant to you. What you've written leaves an identifiable trail—something like your DNA but instead of identifying your biologic self, it identifies your cognitive self. You should think of forensic IRAC as deciphering a code, where each sentence you've written is a clue to piecing together how you approached a problem. It works because when you write, you take the inherently private and internal process called "thought" and make it visible—and provide just the way into your head that we need.

B. Applying the Technique

The first step is to write an MEE answer. Assuming that you've written an answer under timed conditions as part of the Rule of Three, the next step is to put it away. Move on to something else—review your lecture notes, prepare some flash cards, write another essay. You're not ready to be objective about something you've just written. You're too close to see what you've *really* written as opposed to what you *think* you've written. The mind's eye is funny that way: you can read something you've written over and over again and never see the errors because your eye will correct them based on what your mind intended. The only way to overcome this tendency is to distance yourself from your work so you can look at what you've written with a fresh eye and a clear mind. We strongly recommend that you write an essay one day and review it the next.

Sometime the next day, or much, much later that same day, take out the question, and your answer. Re-read the question and then your answer. Now you're ready to proceed. The plan is simple: use IRAC analysis to detect any flaws in that analysis.

As you read your answer, consider each IRAC element against the criteria outlined below. This allows you to evaluate what you've written with the critical eye of a grader and identify your individual strengths and weaknesses. More importantly, by showing you exactly what to look for in each step of an IRAC analysis, you'll be able to pinpoint exactly where in the process any weakness occurs. Then, by following the suggested cures for that particular problem, you'll be able to correct it.

What follows is something like a troubleshooting section in a technical manual where system faults are identified and applicable solutions are provided.

1. *When You Have Trouble Finding the "Issue"*

A failure to properly identify the issue(s) results in a "scattershot" approach in the rest of your answer—a real "hit or miss" situation when it comes to racking up exam points. You may even have written an opening *"The issue is whether"* statement, but it merely restates the interrogatory without articulating the legal question underlying it. As a result, you're misled into thinking you've identified the issue when in fact you've missed it altogether.

Generally, you can tell that you've had difficulty in "spotting the issue" by what you've written in either the rule or the application portion of your answer, or both.

a. **How You Can Tell When It Shows up in Your Statement of the Rule**

When you fail to identify the legal issue, it's likely to turn up as a problem in your statement of the rule. One of the following may occur:

- You may find that the rule discussion is so *general and open-ended* that it completely overlooks the precise rule implicated by the facts.

- Your analysis *glosses* ("sketchy") over the rule so lightly that the grader can't be sure whether you knew the relevant rule or merely happened to mention it.

- You've stated the wrong rule altogether.

Look for examples of the following in the rule section of your essay:

- Lengthy, treatise-like discussions of general legal topics.

  This is a pretty common situation where you've provided lots of "law" but it's too general to address the particular problem implicated by the facts. Typically, what you've managed to do is dance around the topic without engaging it.

  Here, you've decided to show the bar examiners how much time you've spent studying so you display that knowledge by writing everything you know. What happens is that you provide far more information than is necessary, often miss the relevant point, and take up valuable exam time without adding to your grade.

- A rule "dump."

  This may be hard for you to believe but it's not your job to recite all the law you've managed to memorize. We can understand that if you think this way, there's no such thing as a "wrong rule" and the more you write, the better off you'll be. But sorry, it doesn't work like this. Writing about a rule, even if it's correctly stated, is "wrong" if it's not the rule implicated by the facts. More important, you won't receive any points for your efforts and you will waste valuable time.

- A discussion of the "wrong" rule.

  There are a couple of reasons why you might have written the wrong rule (see also the next section on *"When you have trouble writing the "Rule")*, but one very likely reason is that you didn't begin with a proper identification of the issue. It's relatively simple: if you don't define the legal question, how do you know which rule to apply to answer it?

b. How You Can Tell When It Shows up in Your Application

In these cases, your discussion may ramble and roam, moving without any logical transition from topic to topic. Or it may simply repeat the facts from the hypothetical. What's interesting, however, is that a knowledge of substantive law may be indicated by the choice of vocabulary, but since what's written doesn't connect with what's asked in the question, the points gained are very few, if any.

Look for examples of the following in the application portion of your essay:

- No connection between the call-of-the-question and the application section of your answer.

  When you're asked a specific question in a problem, then your analysis must be tailored to that question. For example, if the question asks, *"Was the court correct in admitting testimony of the parties' prior oral agreement?"* then what the grader is probably looking for is an analysis of the parol evidence rule with respect to the facts. If, on the other hand, all you wrote about was the duty of the parties to act in good faith in the performance of the contract, then you've completely ignored the question you were asked to consider.

• Facts in the hypothetical are repeated instead of analyzed.

One very good reason for restating facts instead of analyzing them is failure to work from the legal question. The issue provides focus and direction: it's the "problem" you solve with your "analysis." Without identifying a problem, you have nothing to answer, so you flounder and fall back on narrative.

• A contradiction or discrepancy between what the rule requires and how the facts are analyzed. This problem is best illustrated by an example. Consider the following:

> "Sam agrees to supply Murray Inc. at the end of the growing season in August of this calendar year with all the Spud potatoes that Murray Inc. might require at a price of $100 per ton, delivery included."

You are also told that no specific quantity is stated in the contract but Sam estimates that Murray Inc. would need approximately 30 tons based on what other manufacturers in the area and industry require with similar needs. Because Murray Inc. is getting such a good price for potatoes from Sam, it decides to expand operations suddenly and launch a new product, thereby increasing its demand for potatoes by one-third.

After correctly identifying the issue as one involving a requirements contract and stating the relevant UCC provision, the bar candidate proceeds to discuss a "mutual mistake" in the parties' understanding of how many potatoes would be required. The candidate writes that a mistake was made as to the number of potatoes involved since *"Murray assumed at the time of contract that he would need 40 tons of potatoes but decided after the contract was formed to make a new type of potato chip and would need an additional 20 tons while Same estimated that Murray would need 30 tons."*

This answer is incorrect on several levels:

(i) It is incorrect with respect to the rule at issue because the discussion should focus on whether Murray Inc.'s increased demand was made in "good faith" and whether it was "unreasonably disproportionate" to a stated estimate or comparable requirements;

(ii) It is incorrect with regard to a claim for mutual mistake since the actual number of potatoes could not be a mistake since no number is defined in a requirements contract; and finally, even if it were a mutual mistake, the mistaken belief would have to be held at the time of the contract's formation, not subsequently. Here, the candidate discusses Murray Inc.'s initial assumption about the quantity and then a subsequent increased need. This is not a legal mistake but might be an erroneous prediction about the future.

The problem is that the analysis does not follow the requirements of the rule. Instead, there is a serious disconnect between rule and fact, indicating a genuine lack of understanding.

c. Suggested Remedies

The following is a suggested strategy for identifying the legal issue raised by a hypothetical factual situation.

Summary of steps:

1. Begin your analysis by identifying the call-of-the-question.

2. Articulate the issue based on the interrogatory.

3. Develop an outline of what you need to discuss according to the issue.

Learn to think of the issue as your "legal compass" or, if you prefer a sports analogy, think of it as keeping your "eye on the ball." Either way, what happens when you focus on the issue is that you write strong, effective answers by discussing the right rule and appropriate facts.

Strive to articulate the issue by formulating the legal question presented by the facts. Ask yourself: *"what is the theory"* or *"what is in controversy"* in these facts. That is the issue. Even in jurisdictions that present such open-ended interrogatories as "analyze fully," you must strive to identify the issues and sub-issues as completely as possible in terms of the relevant rules and which facts bring those rules into controversy. This is the only way to ensure that you'll be on the right path in your analysis.

Now let's see how you might do this:

1. Begin your analysis by identifying the call-of-the question.

Does it ask *a specific question,*

- "Is the owner liable to the basket manufacturer for breach of the contract for the aluminum baskets? Is the agent liable? Explain." (Feb 2013)

- "Does Penny have a viable tort claim against the Fernbury Flies? Explain." (Feb 2010)

- "Is the waiver-of-property-rights provision in the premarital agreement enforceable? Explain." (July 2008)

- "Are the profits to be derived from Wendy's songs written after she left Hal subject to division at divorce? Explain." (July 2008)

or does it present a *general question*,

- "How should the assets of the revocable trust be distributed? Explain." (Feb 2015)

- "Is the landlord correct? Explain." (Feb 2013)

- "Is there an enforceable contract against the manufacturer that binds him to sell 10 knives to the chef? Explain." (July 2013)

2. Articulate the issue based on the interrogatory.

    (a) When working with a specific question: identify the legal controversy behind the ruling/ defense/question by asking yourself:

    "What is the theory behind this position?"

Let's look at some examples. Suppose the call-of-the question is something like this:

"Was Ben's decision not to publish Scarlett's book exercised in good faith?"

Do not write as your statement of the issue:

> "The issue is whether Ben's decision was made in good faith."

This is merely a restatement of the question. Instead, you need to review the facts to determine what is in controversy—what are the operative facts—about Ben's decision, i.e., what he did or didn't do in reaching his decision. After carefully reviewing the facts, you'll probably find that the legal "issue" is:

> "The issue is whether Ben exercised good faith in deciding not to publish Scarlett's book when he refused to read the revised manuscript and relied only a preliminary draft."

Let's look at another example. Suppose you're asked the following:

> "Did Ben and Scarlett have an enforceable agreement?"

Once again, your task is not to restate the question but to look closely at the facts to see what is in dispute between the parties regarding the agreement and state something like this:

> "The issue is whether Scarlett's acceptance of Ben's offer to ship the shoes formed a contract when Scarlett's acceptance contained a different delivery date."

By identifying the legal issue as one concerning the formation of a contract when terms in the acceptance varied from the terms of the offer, your discussion of the rule and the facts will turn naturally to the UCC's "battle of the forms" and its difference from the common law's "mirror image rule."

(b)   When working with a general-style question: determine whether you need to identify causes of actions, possible defenses, remedies, etc.

3.   Develop an outline of what you need to discuss according to the issue.

Once you've identified your issue, stay with it and let it guide you through your analysis. By keeping the issue in sight, you'll avoid getting side-tracked and going off on tangents.

(a)   When working with a specific question:

- Each issue forms the basis for a separate IRAC analysis. Still, you must remember that there are usually issues within issues. Each main issue is very likely to break down into sub-issues and each sub-issue gets its own IRAC treatment.

- Outline the rule. List any elements or factors. Note only the exceptions or limitations relevant to your facts. The same is true with defenses. Note only the defenses to be raised based on your facts.

- As you write your analysis, work from your articulation of the rule to guide your application of the facts. Here your rule statement provides a blueprint to follow for your analysis of the facts. You simply match up each element/factor you've identified in the rule with a fact, using the word "because" to make the link between rule and fact.

(b)   When working with a general-style question:

With this type of interrogatory, you've got more work to do but it's not any more of a challenge if you consider the following:

- Use sub-headings to organize your response.

  Your choice of sub-headings should be simple and direct. You can organize your discussion around the parties or causes of action.

- Structure discussions around the issues or defenses.

  If you're working with a fact pattern that's long on issues but short on characters, it's useful to organize around the causes of action.

  This might come up in a criminal or tort problem when you are dealing with one actor who has committed a series of possible crimes or torts. Here, you might consider organizing your analysis around each crime/tort as a way to avoid jumping from one act to another. This ensures that you will focus on one at a time and its attendant elements. You'll want to discuss whether each element is satisfied and whether there are any defenses before moving on to consider another crime/tort.

2.   *When You Have Trouble Writing the "Rule"*

There are two separate and distinct problems which can show up in the rule portion of your exam answer. The first, and by far the most troublesome is where there's a genuine ignorance of the law. You may state the wrong rule or refer to the right rule, but state it incorrectly, either in whole or in part. The second problem occurs when there's a demonstration of substantive knowledge, but it's sketchy and incomplete. Here you don't state "enough" rule to provide an adequate context for analyzing the facts.

No doubt these are both very serious problems. However, while the bar exam grader treats both problems alike with respect to the amount of points lost on your exam, we need to figure out which problem is yours. It makes a difference in how we go about fixing it.

a.   When You Don't Really Know the Applicable Rule

We've repeated this so many times by now that it should come as no surprise to read once again that if you don't *really* know the rule—by which I mean understand it thoroughly, its elements, its consequences, and how it operates—then you can't answer the question correctly and completely. There's no way to fake your way because the language of the law is precise and your explication of the rule must be clear to allow for a meaningful analysis.

First, let's consider an overview of how this problem "presents" and some general "remedies." Then we'll discuss each one in detail to understand how the problem occurs, what it looks like, and consider some specific remedies.

The Overview:

How you can tell

Look for examples of the following in the "rule" section:

- ☐ Substituting your words for legally significant language.

- ☐ Using imprecise language and meaningless phrases.

- ☐ Relying on buzz-words.

- ☐ Failing to use legal terminology, thus sounding as if written by a non-lawyer.

- ☐   Misstating the law.

- ☐   Writing illogical, disjointed statements of the rule.

Look for examples of the following in the "application" section:

- ☐   Narration of the facts instead of analysis.

- ☐   Failure to use any of the following words: "because", "as", "since," "this meant that."

- ☐   Writing logically inconsistent statements.

- ☐   Failing to distinguish between relevant and irrelevant facts.

How you can remedy

There are a number of reasons why you don't know something. The most obvious is that you simply didn't spend enough time studying and memorizing the black letter law. On the other hand, a lack of knowledge can result from an inability to integrate and learn legal principles. Sometimes, you may spend adequate time in study but the time spent is ineffective because you're not focused on the right stuff and in the right way.

In addition to reviewing your notes and memorizing black letter law, you are going to integrate the following tasks into your study plan:

- •   Write "paragraphs of law." By re-writing the rules of law in your own words, you are reducing the applicable law to useable chunks that can be recalled. While it is not necessary to write a rule paragraph for every rule, you should focus on those areas that present the greatest challenge for you. These areas could be difficult because they involve several levels of analysis like a personal jurisdiction analysis or because the subject area is highly technical like Evidence or Secured Transactions.

- Learn to "build a rule" by putting the parts together in a way that forms a logical whole—and in a way that you can remember. This means beginning with a statement of the general rule. Next, define any "legal terms of art" that you referred to in the general statement. Continue to build your rule according to what you need to provide a context for the particular facts of your problem. Typically on an MEE, you will need no more than three sentences of law before you proceed to analyze the facts.

- Practice turning rules into issues and questions. Don't stop at memorizing the definition of a "merchant." Learn to ask yourself, "what's the consequence of finding that the party was a merchant with respect to the transaction in dispute?"

The Specifics:

Now we're ready to get to work. The best way to tell that you really don't know the rule is by checking what you've written for *imprecise or incorrect use of legal language*. When you don't really understand the rule, it "presents" through a failure to use precise legal terminology, incorrect paraphrasing, or the substitution of legal "buzz-words" for legal analysis. Another way a lack of true understanding "presents" is a failure to use legal vocabulary where it would be appropriate and expected. You want to incorporate the basic vocabulary of each subject into how you think and what you write.

(1) Substituting Your Words for Legal Language

The language of the law is precise: change the word and you change the meaning. Not only will you change the meaning, but you'll show the bar examiner in a word (sometimes a single word will betray you) that you've totally disregarded the law and failed to appreciate the special meaning of key language. While it's often necessary to paraphrase, it's essential that you maintain the integrity of the rule by preserving the legally significant language and hence its meaning.

(2) Absence of Legal Vocabulary

Like every other profession, the legal profession has its own specialized language and your job upon entering the field is to speak it fluently and precisely. The bar examiners are looking for evidence in your writing that you have learned the language of the law.

(3) Dependence on "Buzz-Words" Without Back-up

Now that we've told you to use precise legal language, we're going to add a *caveat*: don't substitute legal vocabulary for legal analysis—even when it's the right legal vocabulary. While the right word will carry you far, it won't get you there by itself. When used properly, buzz-words are an appropriate shorthand for conveying information but that must be followed with solid analysis where required—which turns out to be most of the time.

b. When Your Statement of the Rule Is Incomplete or Unorganized

First and foremost, the bar examiners expect your exam answer to demonstrate a firm grasp of black letter law. Quite aside from a sound mastery of legal principles and basic knowledge of core substance, a firm grasp of the law means that you know exactly how much detail is necessary to provide for a meaningful factual discussion. It also means that the law is expressed in a logical and coherent manner.

The Overview:

How you can tell

Look for examples of the following in the "rule" section:

- "Snippets" of law, buzz-words, and catch phrases in place of complete sentences and full explanations.

- Lists of elements without definitions.

- Identification of the relevant exception but no statement of the general rule to provide context.

- Statements of law without a logical connection between them.

How you can remedy

- Follow the building block approach to construct your rule of law

  - *Identify* the general rule that provides the context for the exception.

    - *Explain* the elements in your rule.

    - *Define* the legal terms.

    - Include any relevant *distinctions*, i.e., federal/state or common law/statutory law or majority/minority split.

Look for examples of the following in the "application" section:

- Solid factual discussion that appears element-based but without any explanation or identification of the element.

☐ Analysis of the legally relevant facts but without reference to the supporting legal framework.

☐ Statement of facts but no statement connecting up why that rule is legally significant under these particular facts.

How you can remedy

☐ Build your legal context by working backwards from what you've stated in the facts to determine the scope of the rule necessary to lay a foundation for what you've discussed.

☐ With respect to a fact, ask yourself *why* you found this fact sufficiently relevant to be discussed. This forces you to identify the legal basis for its relevancy.

The Specifics:

The challenge for most students is deciding what to include and not writing too much or too little. The other problem is writing the rule in its logical order. We'll break this down into two steps and begin with writing enough of the rule.

(1) Provide a "General Rule" When It Comes to Writing the Rule

Write enough "rule" to provide the context in which you will analyze the facts. The rule and the facts are inextricably linked. Your analysis of the facts will not make sense unless you have first identified the rule that determines the relevance of those facts.

The question we now need to consider is *"how do you know when your statement of the rule is inadequate, incomplete, and insufficient to do the job?"* It's likely to appear as follows:

- You write "snippets" of law, relying on buzz-words and catch phrases.

- You list elements without explanation or definition.

- You discuss the "exception" without providing the context of the "general rule."

Look for examples of the following in the rule section of your essay:

- Buzz-words and legal phrases instead of completely developed statements of the rule.

- Elements without explanation.

The following is an example of where elements or factors are identified but not otherwise defined. Unless you were to develop each requirement further in the course of your factual analysis, this far too cryptic to serve as the complete recitation of the rule.

There are four elements required to form an agency relationship: a. manifestation of assent; b. subject to control of the principal; c. fiduciary relationship and d. act on his behalf.

Suppose you were given a set of facts and asked to determine whether an agency relationship existed and the *only* information you had to work with was this one sentence. Would you be able to make a determination? As you can see, there are too many gaps in information to allow you to evaluate any facts. After all, you wouldn't know any of the following:

Who has to "manifest assent"?

Assent to what?

What's a principal?

What's a fiduciary?

What does it mean to "act on behalf of another"?

The remedy is simple: include more substance by working from the foundation you've created. If you've listed elements, then define them; if you've identified factors, then explain them. You can include this in your essay either in your "rule paragraph" or by weaving the rule into your factual analysis.

- The "exception" without the "general rule."

If you've identified an exception to a general rule as the critical factor in your problem, then you must also include the general rule. A statement of the general rule provides much-needed context for understanding the exception.

A good example of working from the exception to the general rule are questions that test the Fourth Amendment's prohibition against unreasonable searches and seizures and its corollary, the exclusionary rule. Such questions are not limited to the Fourth Amendment. Given the nature of the law, the list is practically endless: when is there not an exception to a rule? All this means is that when your task is to analyze whether an exception applies, you want to include a statement of the general rule before you turn your attention to the specific exception brought into controversy by the facts of your problem.

Let's consider the following example: a search incident to a valid arrest.

Example: Fourth Amendment and warrantless searches

Don't just write . . .

Pursuant to a lawful arrest, the police officer can make a warrantless search of a vehicle if there is reason to believe it contains contraband.

without including the general rule . . .

Under the Fourth Amendment, a person has the right to be free from unreasonable searches and seizures by the

*government. A search will usually be considered
unreasonable if it is not conducted pursuant to a validly
executed warrant based upon probable cause unless one
of the exceptions applies.*

(2) Write the Rule in Its Logical Order

There is a structure to follow when writing a rule of law. You
should strive to present your statement of the law in its logical
order. This demonstrates your understanding of the material and
makes it easy for the grader to follow. In the process, it helps insure
that you write enough of the law by covering related concepts.

Thoughtful legal analysis requires a logical development and
presentation of the applicable law. The bottom line is that you must
know how a rule breaks down to write it in an organized manner.
You should understand the flow of the rule and how the pieces
connect.

Writing the rule according to its logical order is really just
another way of saying that your writing should be organized. Using
these principles will keep you organized without thinking about it—
follow them and your discussion will be naturally organized.

Consider the following hierarchy of concepts when you write
the rule:

- Move from the general to the specific.

  Begin with a statement of the general rule and move
  to the exception. Moving from the general to the
  specific is simply the natural order of things.

- Define each legal term of art.

  When your statement of the rule contains a legal
  term of art, your next sentence should be a
  definition of that term. This is one of the easiest
  ways to go about building a complete statement of

the rule in a logical manner. The sentences flow almost effortlessly and seamlessly because one statement leads naturally to the next.

3. When You Have Trouble Writing the "Application"

This is by far the simplest problem to correct because the essay has the rules in place but fails to analyze the facts. Clearly, the writer implicitly acknowledged the relevance of the facts or he or she would not have recognized the need to discuss that rule.

The Overview:

How you can tell

Look for examples of the following in the "application" section:

☐   Mere repetition of the facts from the hypothetical.

☐   Conclusory statements.

☐   Reliance on such language as "obviously," "clearly," and "evidently."

☐   Avoiding the question to be analyzed by using "if" and "should." For example, leaving the discussion at stating "*if* the breach was material" instead of evaluating whether or not it was. Or turning the question over to the judge—"*should* the court find that the words constituted a dying declaration"—and then not evaluating whether they were and what consequences would flow from that finding.

☐   There is no mention of any of the individual facts— no use of dates, times, ages, amounts, relationships, locations—nothing that ties the analysis to the specific facts of the problem.

□   Absence of the word "because" or words that serve a similar function like "since," "when," and "as."

How you can remedy

□   Match up each element in the rule to a fact.

□   Use the word "because" to make the connection between rule and fact.

□   Make sure that every conclusion you reach is supported by an explanation of the "why" behind it.

□   Make sure that you "use" every fact of consequence in your analysis. There are very few, if any, red herrings in an MEE question. They are there for a reason. Ask yourself, "Why is this fact here?"

The key in writing the "application" and not simply a recitation of the facts from the hypothetical is to understand that application is analysis. It is explaining the legal significance of each fact. Generally, this is a golden opportunity to rack up exam points because once you've identified the rule, all you have to do is discuss the facts with respect to each of the identified requirements. Some refer to this as a "cut and paste" between the law and the facts or a "matching up" of rule with fact. Either way, the end result is the same: a solid legal analysis.

Let's see how this works.

We'll begin with the most common form of application error—recitation in place of analysis. Recitation occurs when you've simply rewritten the facts that were given to you in the hypothetical. We can change all that with a word.

a.   The Importance of "Because"

Use the word *"because"* to draw the connection between rule and fact. "Because" is the single most important word to use when writing your application. Using the word "because" forces you to make the connection between rule and fact. You'll find that you can also make use of the words "as," "since," and "when"—they often serve the same function as "because."

b. Conclusory Statements

Even if you struggled with "conclusory" statements throughout law school, there is no reason you can't cure the problem for the bar exam—just study the following examples.

What not to write:

The specifications in this agreement are express conditions.

What you should write:

*The specifications in this agreement can be considered express conditions **because** the contract language uses that of express condition **when** it states that the hardwood floor "shall be" of a particular type.*

What not to write:

In addition, Newman will say that the oral agreement contradicts the written agreement which is not allowed under the parol evidence rule.

What you should write:

*In addition, the oral agreement contradicts the written agreement **because** the oral conversation between Ben and Newman allowed Ben to paint the kitchen any time while the written agreement specifies that painting must be done after the cabinetry is completed.*

What not to write:

In this case, Pete the police officer noticed that Dan fit the description of a robbery suspect and arrested him.

What you should write:

*In this case, Pete the police officer realized that Dan fit the description of a robbery suspect, providing probable cause for arrest, **because** Dan had bright red hair, was wearing a green and yellow sweater with purple patches and pointy-toed alligator cowboy boots, fitting the description provided by the eyewitness to the robbery.*

c. Avoiding Analysis with "If"

This is the case where you allude to what needs to be discussed—*if the court finds bad faith*—and then fail to evaluate the conduct. Either you don't know what it means to evaluate the facts or consider the job done by simply referencing them. In either case, it's a point-buster.

This is an easy fix: show all work. Writing an exam answer is like solving a math problem: if you leave out the evaluation, it's like saying that to solve for X, you need to first multiply and then divide—and then not doing it!

C. Making It Visible

Sometimes you just need a way to see the difference between what you wrote and what you should have written—a way to make it visible so it becomes real to you. And you can do this with a few different colored highlighters and the following steps:

1. Write an answer to an MEE question. When you've completed your answer, don't look at it for a few hours or even overnight.

2. When you are ready, gather what you need: your MEE answer, NCBE's Analyses Sheets for that MEE, and a set of color highlighters.

3.   Read through your answer so you see what you've really written, not just what you think you've written.

Assessing substance:

4.   Read through the Analyses Sheets for that MEE, beginning with the identification of Legal Problems (the issues). The Analyses Sheets are all structured the same, beginning with the Legal Problems, following by a Summary of the answer and then a Point by Point breakdown of the issues. The Analyses Sheets are not written as a sample answer, but a guide to the issues, relevant rules, and analysis, together with Notes to the graders where appropriate.

Note: In your self-assessment, do not consider the Analyses Sheets' references to cases, hornbooks, treatises, restatements, etc. These are not expected in a candidate answer but are citations to authority for the grader jurisdictions. Nor should you get lost in the detailed discussions of the rules for different jurisdictions if you are a UBE test-taker. Your task is to state the generally applicable rules of law (i.e., UPC, RUPA, UCC, FRE, FRCP, etc.)

5.   On the Analyses Sheets, begin with the Legal Problems. They are numbered according to the number of issues that should be in the answer. NCBE's numbering scheme may or may not match yours, but it should be close if you followed the question's numbering scheme and/or identified the appropriate issues.

6. Use an orange highlighter to highlight an issue statement or a part of that statement that is not in your answer. Be very specific in noting whether the Analyses Sheet uses the "whether, when" construction and you did not.

7. Use a purple highlighter to highlight every fact that is noted in the Analyses Sheet that is not in your analysis.

8. Use a yellow highlighter for every rule that is in the Analyses Sheet that is not in yours.

9. The colors on the Analyses Sheets make the omissions from your answer visible so you can see what was missing and where.

Assessing format:

10. Now consider your essay's format and structure:

    Use a pink highlighter for the numbers on the Analyses Sheets if they follow the numbering scheme according to the call of the question and you did not.

11. If the MEE does not have numbered questions but a general "Explain fully," then note whether you used sub-headings to organize your answer. There must be some organizational scheme, whether numbers or sub-headings to indicate a structure.

Appendix

The Appendix contains two types of tables. One is organized by bar administration and identifies the MEE subjects tested on a particular bar exam. The other is organized by subject and allows you to focus on individual topics.

A. Table of Issues by Bar Exam Administration

Viewing a bar exam in its entirety lets you see the selection of MEEs on a particular administration and compare administrations over time. *This is not intended to predict what you might expect on your exam, but to show the universe of tested subjects and topics.*

B. Subject Charts

The National Conference of Bar Examiners provides subject matter outlines for each of the MEE subjects.[1] The outlines cover 13 subject areas and the sub-topics within each area. Although there are over 20 pages of identified topics, this need not be as overwhelming as it might seem since we have identified exactly which topics have actually been tested on the essays over the past 14 years.

The individual Subject Charts and NCBE's Subject Matter Outlines for the MEE work together to give you a comprehensive picture of the essay portion of the Uniform Bar Exam. You can see which issues have been tested and how frequently they have been tested. Once again, we must repeat that there is no sure way to predict what will be on the next bar exam. The Subject Charts are not meant to be predictive guides, but study guides: knowing the frequency of some issues allows you to target your study time to where it is most effective.

- Business Associations (Agency and Partnership; Corporations and Limited Liability Companies)

- Civil Procedure

---

[1] *See* National Conference of Bar Examiners, 2018 MEE Subject Matter Outline, http://www.ncbex.org/pdfviewer/?file=%2Fdmsdocument%2F183 (last visited July 16, 2018).

- Conflict of Laws

- Constitutional Law

- Contracts (including Article 2 Sales of the Uniform Commercial Code)

- Criminal Law and Procedure

- Evidence

- Family Law

- Real Property

- Secured Transactions (Article 9 of the Uniform Commercial Code)

- Torts

- Trusts and Estates (Decedents' Estates; Trusts and Future Interests)

Multistate Essay Examination (MEE)

Table of Issues

By Bar Exam Administration: 2005-2018

February 2005 and July 2005

Essay #	February 2005	July 2005
1	Corporations Officer's authority: power of president to hire attorney to initiate action on behalf of corporation (to collect accounts receivable). Authority of corporate officers: acts within scope of ordinary course of business. Authority of board of directors: declaration of dividends, acts in extraordinary course of business.	Decedents' Estates Whether a life insurance beneficiary be changed by a will provision. Joint bank account with right of survivorship; account of convenience, power to write checks only and the intent of the testator. Lapsed legacy: death of beneficiary prior to death of testator, state lapse statute, application of statute to class gifts and to persons who died before will was executed. Uniform Probate Code (UPC) anti-lapse statute compared to common law and state lapse statutes.
2	*Negotiable Instruments/* *No longer on MEE*	Corporations Promoter liability for pre-incorporation contract; promoter as agent in establishing corporation. Novation.

Essay #	February 2005	July 2005
		Factual issue whether promoter would be personally liable based on whether company intended to held promoter liable: can be argued either way. Corporation's ratification or adoption of pre-incorporation contract: express and implied adoption.
3	**Civil Procedure** Jurisdiction: federal subject matter jurisdiction based on diversity of citizenship (28 U.S.C. § 1332(a)); diversity established at the time the suit is filed. Aggregation of claims to satisfy the amount-in-controversy requirement. Federal courts' basis for supplemental jurisdiction under 28 U.S.C. § 1367(a) over all claims that "derive from a common nucleus of operative fact."	**Secured Transactions** Attachment and rights of creditors with unperfected security interests. Creditor's use of self-help remedies to repossess and sell collateral. Foreclosure sale: notice requirement to debtor and "any secondary obligor"; guarantor of loan with actual knowledge of sale but who did not receive proper notice of the sale. Deficiency judgments: secured party fails to comply with foreclosure rules in business transactions, there is a

Essay #	February 2005	July 2005
	Venue: change of venue under 28 U.S.C. § 1404(a) is only permitted to a court where the action could have been brought originally (i.e., where venue was proper at the time suit was filed).	deficiency, and the "rebuttable presumption rule."
4	**Family Law and Conflict of laws** Standards governing custodial parent's relocation: balancing of impact on visitation by noncustodial parent against benefits of the move for the child; "best interests of the child." Enforceability of a registered child support order in a non-issuing state pursuant to the Uniform Interstate Family Support Act (UIFSA). Interstate enforcement and modification of child support orders (UIFSA). Interstate modification of child custody order as governed by Parental	**Family Law** Whether statute of limitations in state's paternity statute violates unwed biological father's substantive due process rights under 14th Amendment. Factors for establishing a significant parental relationship. Presumption of paternity; presumption of legitimacy. Nonparent estopped from disclaiming parental responsibilities when previously consented to act as a parent and support child and child's interests would be harmed by terminating the parental relationship.

Essay #	February 2005	July 2005
	Kidnapping Prevention Act (PKPA) and the Uniform Child Custody Jurisdiction and Enforcement Act (UCCJEA).	Interpreting a state visitation statue: violation of due process of parent when no deference is given to fit parent's determination of best interests of child.
5	**Decedents' Estates** Revocation: physical destruction with intent to revoke; multiple copies of will executed while only 1 copy was destroyed; proponent's burden of proof. Revival of will: destruction of will revives prior will pursuant to state revival statute. Codicil: handwriting and changing a bequest on a previously executed will. Execution requirements: doctrine of dependent relative revocation. Rule of ademption: specific bequest of real property no longer in testator's estate at time	*Negotiable Instruments/ No longer on MEE*

Essay #	February 2005	July 2005
	of death and whether there is entitlement to replacement property.	
6	**Secured Transactions** **UCC Article 9** Unperfected security interest compared to judicial lien creditor. Purchase-money security interest; definition of "goods"; delayed filing and 20-day grace period after delivery of the collateral to perfect by filing, and security interest relating back to the date of the attachment. Item of sale changing from "goods" to a "fixture" (an oven). Priority of liens: competing security interests, judgment liens, mortgages, "fixture filing."	**Civil Procedure** Standard for granting TRO under FRCP 65(b) (to enjoin employee from violating the non-compete provision in contract and disclosing trade secrets). Standard for granting preliminary injunction: (1) risk of "irreparable harm" to plaintiff if preliminary injunction is not granted; (2) likelihood of plaintiff's success on the merits of the underlying claim; (3) "balance of the equities"— likelihood that the harm the plaintiff will suffer in the absence of the preliminary injunction outweighs the harm the defendant will suffer if it is granted; (4) the public interest. A mandatory injunction: order compelling party to engage in particular acts.

Essay #	February 2005	July 2005
7	**Agency** Defining the agency relationship. Undisclosed principals and liability of undisclosed principal for contracts (purchase of supplies and employment contract) entered into by general agent in violation of principal's instructions. Types of authority: actual, inherent, and apparent authority.	**Trusts and Future Interests** Testamentary trust. Elements of a valid trust: definite beneficiaries required; trust established to give income to "my friends" invalid for want of definite beneficiaries. Donee's exercise of special power of appointment to appoint trust assets (principal) and to create more limited interests (life estate). Special power of appointment exercised in favor of an impermissible object. Partially ineffective exercise of special power of appointment and consequences to permissible object.

February 2006 and July 2006

Essay #	February 2006	July 2006
1	**Trusts and Future Interests** Elements of a valid trust: trustee, beneficiary, and trust property. Revocable trust. Trust written on a napkin with intention to fund it at a later date: trust arises when funded. Pour-over will to a trust where the trust's terms were incorporated in a writing (napkin) that was written before the will. Incorporation by reference doctrine: testamentary additions to revocable trust. Self-settled trusts; enforceability of spendthrift provision; reach by settlor's creditors to trust assets of revocable trust.	*Negotiable Instruments/ No longer on MEE*

Essay #	February 2006	July 2006
2	**Agency**	**Agency and Partnership**
	Vicarious liability of employer for acts of employees committed within the scope of employment. Defining the agency relationship: reflected in master-servant relationship. Factors distinguishing between independent contractor and employer/employee. Fiduciary duties of agent/employee: duty to obey reasonable instructions and duty to act solely for benefit of principal.	Definition of partnership: determining whether parties are partners based on a loan to the partnership (no) but forgiveness of the loan in exchange of share of the profits (yes). Partner as agent of partnership: partner's authority to bind partnership for an act for carrying on the ordinary course of partnership business, but not for an act outside the ordinary business. Actual and apparent authority. Partners' joint and several liability for partnership obligations.
3	**Civil Procedure**	**Decedents' Estates**
	Jurisdiction: federal subject matter jurisdiction based on anticipation of a federal	When a joint will constitutes a will contract: determined by language used, "each of us agrees" is a contract between

Essay #	February 2006	July 2006
	defense; "well-pleaded complaint rule." Jurisdiction: federal subject matter jurisdiction based on diversity of citizenship (28 U.S.C. § 1332(a): determining domicile based on residence and "intent to remain." FRCP 4(k)(1): asserting personal jurisdiction over a non-resident defendant. Exercise of state's long-arm statute where it extends jurisdiction as far as the Due Process Clause of the 14th Amendment allows; evaluation of internet-based contacts.	husband and wife; contract becomes irrevocable at death of first spouse; includes property acquired after death of a spouse; beneficiaries of joint will as contract creditors of surviving spouse's estate. Doctrine of "facts of independent significance" and rule of construction that wills "speak at the time of death." Incorporation by reference: document executed after will executed as compared to a document in existence prior to the execution of a will; invalid bequest not evidenced by a testamentary instrument.
4	**Family Law** Validity of common law marriage in states that do not recognize common law marriages.	**Family Law and Conflict of Laws** Common law marriage elements. Validity of common law marriage in states that do

Essay #	February 2006	July 2006
	Requirements to establish a common law marriage. Whether agreements between cohabitants establish property or support rights ("ceremony of commitment"). Protection under the due process clause of 14th Amendment for unwed father who lived with his child for a substantial portion of his child's life and wishes to maintain an active, custodial relationship with the child; his parental rights cannot be severed without his consent or showing of parental unfitness.	not recognize common law marriages. Mutual vows, ceremony of commitment and enforceable agreement to share property, verbal cohabitation agreement. Termination of parental rights of unwed father, adoption without consent of father, due process, 14th Amendment, involved father who lived with his child for a substantial portion of his child's life, and who wishes to maintain an active, custodial relationship with the child.
5	Corporations Authority of board of directors to call a special meeting of shareholders. What constitutes proper notice for a special shareholder meeting.	Corporations Breach of fiduciary duty of majority shareholder for failure to disclose material information to minority shareholders; what

Essay #	February 2006	July 2006
	Voting rights of different classes of stock: conditions imposed on voting rights by articles of incorporation. Proxy agreements: definition; requirements for a proper appointment. Quorum requirements: majority needed to dissolve corporation.	constitutes material information. Duty of care and business judgment rule in approving a merger. Duty of fair dealing when a majority shareholder purchases the interest of the minority shareholders.
6	**Secured Transactions** **UCC Article 9** Consignment agreement: where consignor retains title to goods. Collateral in inventory: creditor of a consignee "deemed to have rights and title to goods identical" to those of consignor. Purchase-money security interest in inventory held by a consignor of goods. Priority of liens: competing security interests.	**Civil Procedure** Amended pleadings: complaint may be amended "once as a matter of course at any time before a responsive pleading is served" under FRCP 15(a) and will "relate back to the date of the original pleading" if requirements of FRCP 15(c) are met. Complaint amended after statute of limitations had run to correct a mistake in the name of a defendant. Final judgment rule; consideration of statutory

Essay #	February 2006	July 2006
	Perfection of a security interest; financing statement; notification requirements.	and judge-made exceptions, including the collateral order exception. FRCP 16(a) and (f): pre-trial conferences and court's power to sanction a party for party's attorney for failure to appear. Where entry of default judgment may be an abuse of discretion.
7	Decedents' Estates Advancement: whether inter vivos gift by donor is an advancement on the beneficiary's legacy; intention of the testator. Slayer statute: felonious intent and killing of decedent compared to negligence as cause of testator's death. Intestacy distribution incorporated in will. Per capita distribution of assets compared to per stirpes distribution of assets.	Secured Transactions Improper disposition of the collateral (consumer goods); public v. private disposition of collateral; "commercially reasonable" manner; notice of sale. Remedies of consumer as a result of secured party's failure to provide notice of disposition and a "commercially reasonable" disposition of collateral; actual damages, statutory damages, right of redemption, Deficiency judgments: secured party fails to comply with foreclosure

Essay #	February 2006	July 2006
		rules in a consumer transaction, liability of the debtor, "absolute bar" rule, and "rebuttable presumption rule."

February 2007 and July 2007

Essay #	February 2007	July 2007
1	*Negotiable Instruments/ No longer on MEE*	**Contracts** Requirements for an enforceable contract: offer, acceptance, consideration and, when required, a signed writing. Requirements for an offer; distinguishing between a counteroffer and an inquiry. Rules for acceptance: when is acceptance effective upon dispatch, the "mailbox rule"; rejection effective upon receipt. Rule where an acceptance is sent after a rejection: the one to reach the recipient first is effective. Statute of Frauds: one-year provision. Personal services contract: damages are available but specific performance is not.

Essay #	February 2007	July 2007
2	**Trusts and Future Interests** Testamentary trust. Elements of a valid trust: a trust established to give income to "my friends" fails because it lacks definite beneficiaries. Distribution of trust income to residuary legatee when trust fails; whether to accumulate trust income for ultimate distribution to remainder beneficiaries or currently distribute income to presumptive remainder beneficiaries. Creditor's right to reach trust income when trust contains no spendthrift provision. Rights of creditors no greater than rights of beneficiary. Bequest to charity that no longer exits: cy *pres*	**Civil Procedure** Removal from state court to federal court; determining citizenship of executor for diversity and removal purposes. Preclusive effect of default judgment when court had subject matter and personal jurisdiction. FRCP 13(a): compulsory counterclaim requirement.

Essay #	February 2007	July 2007
	doctrine, general charitable intent.	
3	**Civil Procedure** Discovery: determining what is discoverable. Plaintiff served requests for production of documents in personal injury action seeking investigative and accident reports and the bus driver's entire personnel file, including safety and driving records and disciplinary records. FRCP 26 (b)(1): "documents relevant to a claim or defense." FRCP 26 (b)(3): materials "prepared in anticipation of litigation."	**Family Law** Basis for setting aside or modifying a divorce settlement or agreement before a final divorce judgment is entered: when a spouse's coercive behavior, fraud, or duress results in a substantively unfair agreement. Setting aside a divorce settlement agreement based on serious misconduct by the mediator. Factors for determining spousal maintenance award: contributions to marriage, duration of marriage, parties' financial resources and needs.
4	**Family Law and Conflict of Laws** Jurisdiction and divorce: over the marriage and over the property.	**Agency and Partnership** Definition of partnership: intent to form a partnership; written agreement not required.

Essay #	February 2007	July 2007
	A court's jurisdiction to grant its domiciliary's divorce petition as long as the state's jurisdictional requirements are satisfied. Divisible divorce: a court's jurisdiction in an *ex parte* divorce extends to the marriage only and not to the property of the marriage. Personal jurisdiction over both spouses needed for property division order. No-fault divorce granted based on separation and irreconcilable differences; does not matter whether the separation was nonconsensual or one spouse is seeking to reconcile. Separate property and marital property.	Partner as agent of partnership: partner's authority to bind partnership for an act for carrying on the ordinary course of partnership business; acts outside the ordinary course of business require consent of all partners. Actual and apparent authority. A partner is jointly and severally liable for partnership obligations; partner liability includes unpaid wages of an employee. Personal liability of general partner and limited partners for partnership's debts. Procedure for recovering against partners personally: judgment must first be obtained individually against each partner and against the partnership and levy

Essay #	February 2007	July 2007
		execution against partnership assets.
5	**Decedents' Estates** Effect of a stock dividend or stock split on a specific bequest of "my 100 shares"; common law compared to the Uniform Probate Code (UPC). Disclaimer of legacy: sister of testator disclaims: beneficiary deemed to have failed to survive testator, lapsed legacy, anti-lapse statute. Advancement: whether the inter vivos gift by donor is an advancement on the beneficiary's legacy; intention of the testator. Abatement of legacies in order of the classification of legacy.	**Criminal Law** Second-degree murder (shot friend while aiming at lamp behind friend). *Mens rea*, "malice aforethought", "depraved-heart" murder. "Extreme indifference to value of human life", reckless behavior. Causation: defendant's acts must be both the actual ("but for") and proximate cause of death. A "dependent intervening cause", a consequence of defendant's prior wrongful conduct, breaks the chain of causation when it is bizarre or out of the ordinary.
6	**Agency and Partnership** Limited partnership. Right of limited partners to obtain information	**Real Property** Requirements for a valid deed (grantee must be identified).

Essay #	February 2007	July 2007
	from general partner regarding the financial condition of the business upon "reasonable demand": tax returns, contracts, correspondence. Liability of limited partners in a limited liability partnership: generally not liable for the obligations of a limited partnership unless participate in the "control of the business." "Safe harbor": RULPA's list of activities that do not constitute the exercise of control of the business includes removal of a general partner. Participation in control of business can make limited partners liable for obligations of limited partnership under certain circumstances.	Adverse possession: elements. Adverse possessor's claim to possession against subsequent BFP. State recording statute and its effect on owner who acquired land by adverse possession (where owner had no deed to record).

Essay #	February 2007	July 2007
7	**Secured Transactions UCC Article 9** Perfection of a security interest in accounts receivable. Errors in UCC filing statements: ineffective filing of financing statement where the name of debtor is incorrect (trade name as opposed to the name of the corporation), "seriously misleading" test", search of records would not disclose the financing statement. Automatic perfection of security interest in accounts (upon attachment); when assignment of accounts do not transfer "significant part of assignor's outstanding accounts." Priority of liens: competing security interests and "first to file or perfect rule."	*Negotiable Instruments/ No longer on MEE*

Essay #	February 2007	July 2007
8	*No question*	**Trusts** Drafting of trust agreement to reflect Settlor's intent. MEE task requires comparing list of Settlor's goals in creating the trust to the Trust Agreement drafted by the attorney and making changes to meet the Settlor's stated goals. Settlor wants full control of trust assets in memo: Settlor should retain power to revoke, to withdraw principal; Settlor should be named as sole trustee. Trust should include an additions clause. Ascertainable standard for distributions of trust principal to wife and beneficiary's right to withdrawal of trust principal so that wife is comfortably provided for. Special testamentary power of appointment created by trust so that

Essay #	February 2007	July 2007
		wife can reward her children in her will. Drafting using the term "issue" to ensure child that predeceases wife will take the deceased child's share of trust principal. Anti-lapse statutes and how they apply to inter vivos trusts as compared to testamentary trusts.
9	*No question*	**Corporations and LLCs** Members' right (of a manager-managed LLC) to maintain an action against manager of LLC for mismanagement: derivative action vs. direct action. Procedural requirements for bringing a derivative action (set forth in ULLCA). Members of LLC right to bring a derivative action on behalf of LLC for mismanagement. What constitutes a violation of manager's fiduciary duty of care:

Essay #	February 2007	July 2007
		negligence standards; simple negligence, gross negligence. Business judgment rule. Personal liability of LLC members for negligence. Piercing the LLC veil to hold members personally liable: "mere instrumentality" or "unity of interest and ownership."

February 2008 and July 2008

Essay #	February 2008	July 2008
1	**Decedents' Estates** Grounds for contesting a will: elements for undue influence. Effect of finding of undue influence: can invalidate all or a portion of the will. Rules of intestacy are followed upon invalidation of a will. When a residuary bequest fails, does the invalidated share pass to the testator's heirs or to the remaining residuary legatees: common law approach—"no residue of residue" rule (testator's heirs) compared to UPC approach—"residue of residue" rule (other residuary legatee)	**Secured Transactions** **UCC Article 9** Perfection of a security interest; inventory and equipment; after acquired collateral. Motor vehicles: certificate of title statute and notation on certificate of title as perfection of a security interest as compared to filing a financing statement. Priority of liens: competing security interests. Continuation of security interest: accessions, priority rules governing accessions with certificate of title statutes; description of the collateral in creditor's security agreement. Purchase-money security interest in equipment takes priority over competing security

Essay #	February 2008	July 2008
		interest which was acquired earlier in time.
2	**Torts** Strict products liability (food poisoning): liability of commercial product sellers compared to occasional, non-commercial food seller. Defective products: where a product's risk of being unreasonably dangerous cannot be eliminated, adequate warnings or instructions are required or the product is defective. Negligence: where there are multiple defendants and cannot show which of three parties acted negligently because parties acted independently and not jointly. Where *res ipsa loquitur*, alternative liability, and joint enterprise liability are unavailable to	**Constitutional Law** First Amendment: freedom of the press. Defamation: public figure, "actual malice", "reckless disregard" of the truth. Freedom of the press: lack of immunity for breaking the law or committing a tort. Invasion of privacy: lawfully obtained information involving a matter of public concern, reasonable expectation of privacy.

Essay #	February 2008	July 2008
	support a negligence claim.	
3	**Family Law** Meaning of an adoption order; whether an adoptive parent can dissolve the adoption when the parent quarrels frequently with the child. Seeking a retroactive modification of child support obligation: forbidden by federal law. Voluntary reduction of income not a basis to obtain downward modification of child support obligation unless made in good faith and without incurring hardship on child. Must show a "substantial change in circumstances" to obtain modification of future support obligation. Support of children of employable age; compliance with	**Agency and Partnership** Identifying partnership property. Whether partnership property is subject to attachment and execution by judgment creditor of individual partner. How creditor of individual partner can collect from a partner's financial interest in a partnership. Assignment of partnership interest: rights of assignee (financial interest only). Types of partnerships: partnership for term, partnership at will, or partnership for a particular undertaking; how type of partnership affects a forced dissolution.

Essay #	February 2008	July 2008
	reasonable parental demands.	
4	**Evidence** Hearsay; exceptions to hearsay. Business-records exception; statements made for purpose of receiving medical diagnosis or treatment. Two evidentiary privileges applicable to the marital relationship: testimonial spousal privilege and marital confidential communications privilege. Hearsay admissible to impeach hearsay declarant's credibility.	**Real Property** Landlord/tenant: creating periodic and at-will tenancies. Statute of Frauds: one-year provision (3 years in some jurisdictions). Violation of statute of frauds, possession of property and acceptance of rent, creation of at-will or periodic tenancy, month-to month tenancy. Terminating at-will and periodic tenancies: notice requirements. Assignment of lease that is silent about assignments, liability for rent of assignor and assignee.
5	**Corporations** Corporate officer and director's duty of loyalty to corporation. Safe harbors for director who breaches his duty of loyalty: approval by	**Civil Procedure** FRCP 19: joinder of a "necessary party." FRCP 13(a): defendant's counterclaim against plaintiff is compulsory when it arises from the

Essay #	February 2008	July 2008
	disinterested directors, approval by disinterested shareholders, or fairness (RMBCA). Duty of board of directors to act on an informed basis when reviewing a contract in which a director has an interest. Business judgment rule; duty of care.	"same transaction or occurrence." Federal courts' basis for supplemental jurisdiction under 28 U.S.C. § 1367(a) over all claims that "derive from a common nucleus of operative fact" (unpaid $50 restaurant bill).
6	**Civil Procedure** FRCP 50(b): judgment as a matter of law ("JMOL", also called a judgment notwithstanding the verdict, "JNOV"); when the motion must be brought. FRCP 50(a): standard for granting a motion for JMOV. FRCP 59(b): procedure for filing a motion for a new trial and the "miscarriage of justice" standard for granting it.	**Trusts** Revocable trust. Validity of pour-over will assets to a trust created during testator's lifetime either by testator or another. Validity of additions to revocable trust which was amended after will is executed. Incorporation-by-reference. Construction of a trust amendment with two possible interpretations: grantor's intent regarding

Essay #	February 2008	July 2008
	Juror misconduct: challenge based on bias and nondisclosure during *voir dire*.	age and survivorship contingencies. Whether grandchild is a substituted taker when trust instrument specifies "children" and includes words of survivorship ("who are living"). Anti-lapse statutes and application to wills as opposed to trusts.
7	**Secured Transactions UCC Article 9** Perfection of a security interest in deposit or demand accounts: secured party must have control of the account to perfect their interest. Errors in UCC finance statements; effective filing of financing statement where the name of debtor was incorrect; "seriously misleading" test; search of records would disclose financing statement.	**Family Law and Conflict of Laws** Which state law determines enforceability of a premarital agreement: law of state where contract is signed or law of state with which parties have the "most significant relationship." Determining enforceability of premarital agreement governing property distribution: voluntariness, unconscionability, reasonable disclosure of assets and liabilities. Premarital agreement regarding child support or

Essay #	February 2008	July 2008
	Priority of liens: competing security interests.	custody is unenforceable if it is not in the "best interests of the child." Separate and marital property; in a majority of states, marital property continues to accrue until final divorce decree.
8	**Criminal Law and Procedure** Fourth Amendment: determining a "seizure" and whether that seizure was reasonable under the Fourth Amendment. Exclusionary rule and "fruit of the poisonous tree." Questioning of suspect when there is a "reasonable articulable suspicion." *Miranda* rights: determining when they attach (suspect is subject to an in-custody interrogation). When is a subject "in custody."	**Contracts** Calculating damages in breach of contract: cost-of-completion v. difference in value. Award of consequential damages: test of foreseeability. Damages must be calculable with reasonable certainty to be recoverable (calculation difficulties with respect to a new business). Calculation of damage award includes subtraction of costs avoided by not having to perform; reduction of award to present value when assessing damages based

Essay #	February 2008	July 2008
	Voluntary confession compared to an involuntary confession.	on loss of future income; duty to mitigate damages.
9	**Trusts** Irrevocable trust. Duties of trustee with respect to management of trust. Duty of loyalty: investing in a corporation where the trustee has a substantial investment. Duty to invest prudently: investing in closely held corporation that was "cash poor." Duty to diversify trust investments: investing 90% of trust assets in two corporations that were extremely similar and had same market risks. Duty of care: investing in items that did not earn income and were not liquid so income beneficiary received nothing and prevented beneficiary from	*Negotiable Instruments/* *No longer on MEE*

Essay #	February 2008	July 2008
	withdrawing trust principal as provided for in the terms of the trust.	

February 2009 and July 2009

Essay #	February 2009	July 2009
1	**Agency** Defining the agency relationship (consulting contract). Power of agent to bind principal (to a contract). Actual and apparent authority. Agent exceeding authority or acting without authority and consequences.	**Trusts** Irrevocable trust. Trustee with absolute and uncontrolled discretion to distribute income and principal; abuse of discretion by failing to distribute income based upon personal motives; disagreement with beneficiary's political opinions. Duty of loyalty: self-dealing; purchasing assets from the trust without court approval; no appraisal but purchased by trustee at fair market value. Bequest to charity that no longer exists: *cy pres* doctrine, general charitable intent.
2	**Evidence** FRE 404: character evidence. Impeachment of witness on cross-examination	**Constitutional Law** First Amendment: freedom of speech. Sedition Statute: inciting illegal conduct must meet

Essay #	February 2009	July 2009
	with a specific instance of prior bad act about lying on job application. FRE 608(b): forbids use of extrinsic evidence to impeach witness's character for truthfulness. FRE 612: only counsel for opposing party can offer document to refresh recollection of a witness.	"imminent and likely" test under *Brandenburg*. Abusive Words Statute: "fighting words" are unprotected speech when likely to cause a violent reaction. Statutes may be overbroad where it punishes speech that is merely rude or abusive because it reaches protected speech. Commentary on matters of public concern are afforded the highest level of First Amendment protection.
3	**Decedents' Estates** Distribution of assets in will. Effect of stock dividend or stock split on a specific bequest of "my 100 shares." Rule of ademption: specific bequest of real property no longer in testator's estate at time	**Family Law and Conflict of Laws** Interstate enforcement and modification of child support orders (Uniform Interstate Family Support Act (UIFSA). Enforcement of registered child support order in non-issuing state even when non-issuing state lacks

Essay #	February 2009	July 2009
	of death, replacement property. Generically described property in a will, "my automobile" does not follow rule of ademption when a different car is owned at time of death. Disclaimer of legacy: friend disclaims and beneficiary deemed to have failed to survive the testator, lapsed legacy, anti-lapse statute.	personal jurisdiction over respondent (UIFSA). Under federal Parental Kidnapping Prevention Act (PKPA), only issuing jurisdiction can modify child custody order so long as child or any contestant continues to reside in that state and issuing states does not decline to exercise jurisdiction. Custody modification based on a "substantial change in circumstances": whether parental relocation qualifies as such a change; consideration of "best interests of the child." Modification of child support obligation; may not be modified retroactively, but may be modified prospectively if there is a "substantial change in circumstances" that significantly reduces the child's need or the obligor's ability to pay.

Essay #	February 2009	July 2009
4	**Real Property** Tenancy in common: statutory presumption when conveyance to 2 or more grantees. Joint tenancy: 4 unities test (common law); is a joint tenancy or tenancy-in-common created when a deed's language includes "jointly" and "equally, to share and share equally" but does not mention survivorship? Act and consequence of severing a joint tenancy: mortgage by one joint tenant, contract to sell by one joint tenant. Distinction between "lien theory" and "title theory" jurisdictions. Bona fide purchaser for value; recording of mortgagee gives constructive notice to purchasers regardless of unrecorded deed.	**Secured Transactions** UCC Article 9 Security interest in equipment; after acquired collateral. Agreement that is called a lease may be a security interest: "economic realities" of the transaction where lessee has option to become owner with a nominal payment at end of the lease. Perfection of a security interest. Creditor's use of self-help remedies to repossess and sell collateral. Priority of liens: competing security interests. Applying proceeds of sale towards competing interests. Good faith purchaser of collateral at foreclosure sale: "transferee for value."

Essay #	February 2009	July 2009
	Doctrine of equitable conversion.	
5	**Civil Procedure and Conflict of Laws** FRCP 4 and Due Process clause of U.S. Constitution: evaluating basis for email service of process on a foreign corporation. Action against a foreign corporation on federal law claim and state law claim. Federal court sitting in diversity must apply choice-of-law rule of the state in which court sits when there is non-federal claim. Restatement (Second) of Conflict of Laws § 145: applying choice of law rules to an issue in tort (unfair competition).	**Contracts** Consideration: requirement of a "bargained-for exchange." Past consideration or past performance. Substitutes for consideration: material benefit rule and promissory estoppel.

Essay #	February 2009	July 2009
6	*Negotiable Instruments/ No longer on MEE*	**Civil Procedure** Process for removing a case from state court to federal court. FRCP 20: joinder of claims in "same transaction or occurrence" and "common questions of law and fact." Subject matter jurisdiction. Diversity jurisdiction. Supplemental jurisdiction statute 28 U.S.C. § 1367; claims arising out of state law; "common nucleus of operative fact" test.
7	**Torts** Negligence: standard of care owed by tenant to tenant's guest; standard for 8-year old child. Contributory negligence/comparative negligence. Negligence *per se*, state statute to keep apartment in good repair.	**Criminal Law and Procedure** Fourth Amendment: standing to challenge the legality of a search, reasonable expectation of privacy. Attempted robbery: elements, intention & actions "beyond mere preparation." Defense of voluntary withdrawal or

Essay #	February 2009	July 2009
	Causation, proximate cause of injuries, intervening causes to break chain of causation.	abandonment of crime when actions go beyond mere preparation.
8	**Family Law** Due process requirements for assertion of personal jurisdiction over a nonresident parent in a child support action. State long-arm statute in fact pattern same as in Uniform Interstate Family Support Act (UIFSA). Contract to waive Dad's child support duty unenforceable because inconsistent with "best interest of child." Calculation of child support based upon income and earnings of parents, not public assistance levels. Child custody and visitation determination, "best interest of child" standard.	**Partnership** Determining type of entity: limited partnership or general partnership when no general partner signs the limited partnership agreement. Partner liability for partnership obligations or debt; partners jointly and severally liable. Procedure for recovering against partners personally: judgment must first be obtained individually against each partner and against the partnership and levy execution against partnership assets. Partner liability for tort (wrongful death); joint and several liability.

Essay #	February 2009	July 2009
9	**Corporations** When directors are entitled to the protection of the business judgment rule. Directors' duty to become informed before making business decisions. Breach of duty of care; breach of duty of loyalty. Director's failure to disclose his interest in a transaction to the other directors. Exculpatory provisions in articles of incorporation shielding directors from liability in money damages for failure to exercise adequate care in performance of their duties as directors.	**Decedents' Estates** Grounds for contesting a will: elements for undue influence, elements for fraud in the execution (misrepresents character/contents of the instrument) and in the inducement. Effect of finding of undue influence: can invalidate all or a portion of the will. General power of appointment and the proper exercise of power; residuary clause in will that makes no mention of power of appointment. Simultaneous Death Act: common accident where beneficiary survives testator by 1 week. Intestacy distribution rules: whether testator's niece or testator's uncle take if will is declared invalid. Parentelic method (UPC approach) of determining heirship compared to intestacy

Essay #	February 2009	July 2009
		schemes governed by the civil law consanguinity method (minority method).

February 2010 and July 2010

Essay #	February 2010	July 2010
1	**Secured Transactions** UCC Article 9 Security interest in inventory. Retention of title by seller of delivered goods until payment is made is ineffective, resulting in an unperfected security interest in goods rather than a retention of title. Perfecting a security interest in inventory: raw materials as inventory. Priority of liens: competing security interests, perfected v. unperfected. Attachment of security interest, debtor must have "rights in collateral" (undelivered goods.)	**Agency and Partnership** Partnership formation (general partnership) without a partnership agreement or formalities of other types of partnerships. Investment with a return of profits and with intention to form a partnership; compared to a loan with the right to receive profits until loan is paid in full. Assignment of partnership interest and rights of assignee to receive profits. Rights of assignee to inspect books and records and participate in management of partnership. Identifying partnership property and the misuse of partnership property by a partner.

Essay #	February 2010	July 2010
2	**Real Property** Types of easements. Actual notice, constructive notice, or inquiry notice with regard to easements which are visible (power lines) and easements which are not visible (underground gas lines), when the easements are not recorded and when there are subsequent purchasers for value. "Shelter doctrine." Conveyance by full covenant and warranty deed: covenant against encumbrances.	**Contracts/Article 2** UCC Article 2 sale of goods. Breach of warranty—creation of express warranty through affirmations of fact relating to the goods that are part of the basis of the bargain. Misrepresentation as common law basis to avoid or rescind the contract; common law principles supplement the Code under UCC § 1-103. Revocation of acceptance; duty to inspect and difficulty of discovery of latent defects. Damages: recovery of contract price and incidental and consequential damages; alternative remedy of "cover" damages. *Negotiable Instruments/ No longer on MEE*

Essay #	February 2010	July 2010
3	**Family Law**	**Decedents' Estates**
	Basis for setting aside a settlement agreement before a final divorce judgment is entered: if fraud, overreaching, or duress results in a substantively unfair agreement.	Execution requirements of a will: doctrine of integration for multi-page will (validity when all pages of will are together but unstapled).
	Consideration of marital misconduct in property or alimony determination; distinction between marital misconduct and financial misconduct in award considerations.	Codicil: effect of handwritten change to bequest on a previously executed will.
	Marital and separate property: professional license (law degree is marital property only in NY) acquired during the course of the marriage.	Doctrine of dependent relative revocation (revocation based on mistaken assumption of law or fact is ineffective if testator would not have revoked if he had accurate information).
	Rehabilitative award for spousal support and maintenance; factors in determining spousal support and maintenance (alimony) awards.	Bequest to "my children" when testator intended only biological children to take under the will; rights of adopted and non-marital child.
		Reformation of a will: use of extrinsic evidence to correct a mistake.

Essay #	February 2010	July 2010
4	**Torts** Battery: intent and knowledge to a substantial certainty (pedestrian hit by a baseball that traveled over fence at baseball stadium). Negligence. Vicarious liability of employer for negligence of employee. Custom: industry standards in profession in determining negligence. "Eggshell skull."	**Constitutional Law** First Amendment and types of forums: public forum, limited public forum and nonpublic forum. Public forum: content-neutral regulation must meet intermediate scrutiny (statute preventing leaflet distribution on a public street). Limited public forum: rules applicable to traditional public forum apply; no exception to requirement of content neutrality when religious speech is at issue. Non-public forum: state can regulate conduct without communicative value in a nonpublic forum.
5	**Corporations** Closely held corporation. Shareholder's right of inspection of corporation's books and records (proper purpose	**Real Property** Terms of conveyance ambiguous: fee simple on condition subsequent or fee simple determinable and the consequences that arise from each.

Essay #	February 2010	July 2010
	of valuing shares of corporation). Shareholder's right to dividends; whether a suit to compel payment of a dividend is a suit to enforce a right of the corporation or a suit to enforce an individual right of the shareholder. Business judgment rule.	Interpreting grantor's intent: preference for fee simple on condition subsequent. Future interest and interpreting a state statute which allows interest to pass by will; interpreting a will with a survivorship contingency of "my surviving children" where one child predeceases testator.
6	**Civil Procedure** Subject matter jurisdiction. Jurisdiction: federal subject matter jurisdiction based on diversity of citizenship and amount-in-controversy requirement (28 U.S.C. § 1332(a)). Determining citizenship of corporation and permanent resident alien for diversity purposes.	**Family Law** Determining enforceability of premarital agreement governing property distribution: voluntariness, unconscionability, reasonable disclosure of assets and liabilities. Marital and separate property: property acquired during marriage and by gift; pension can be part marital and part separate property. Alimony: financial resources, marital contributions and marital

Essay #	February 2010	July 2010
	Diversity jurisdiction in breach of contract case (insurance policy). Domestic relations exception to federal courts' exercise of diversity jurisdiction: federal courts will not exercise jurisdiction over cases that are primarily marital disputes. FRCP 20: joinder of claims in "same transaction or occurrence" and "common questions of law and fact"; the logical-relationship test.	duration, spousal misconduct, injured spouse.
7	**Evidence** Admissibility of relevant evidence in negligence action. FRE 701: non-expert opinion evidence. FRE 404(a): evidence of character trait not admissible for proving action in conformity on a particular occasion.	**Civil Procedure** FRCP 4(k)(1): asserting personal jurisdiction over a non-resident defendant. Exercise of state's long-arm statute where it extends jurisdiction as far as the Due Process Clause of the 14th Amendment allows; evaluation of contacts with forum state for finding of specific

Essay #	February 2010	July 2010
	FRE 406: habit evidence (cell phone usage). Relevancy of memory loss concerning events related to the incident. FRE 401-403: where parties have stipulated to injuries, evidence of additional injuries not mentioned in stipulation are inadmissible as waste of time and may be unfairly prejudicial.	jurisdiction based on nonresident's purposeful availment of benefits of forum state and foreseeability of being haled into court. Jurisdiction: federal subject matter jurisdiction based on diversity of citizenship and amount-in-controversy requirement (28 U.S.C. § 1332(a)). Determining citizenship of corporation for diversity purposes. Determining domicile based on residence and "intent to remain"; satisfying the amount-in-controversy requirement. Determining whether federal-question jurisdiction exists: whether claims alleged in complaint are created by federal or state law (federal statute, but state law claim).

Essay #	February 2010	July 2010
8	**Trusts** Revocable trust. After-born children: "surviving children" as a class does not close until Settlor's death and would include "after-born" children. Distribution of trust assets where remainderman predeceases the life tenant: follow the directives in trust instrument; outcome different under UPC where survivors take a predeceased person's share by representation. Disclaimer of interest in a trust by beneficiary: beneficiary deemed to predecease the Settlor; different result under UPC's survivorship rule. Trustee's duty to invest prudently. Duty of fiduciary of a revocable trust who is acting in accordance with	**Criminal Law** Larceny by false pretenses: elements. *Actus reus* and m*ens rea* elements of false pretenses. False statements of a material fact compared to commercial puffery. False statements made knowingly with the intent to defraud.

Essay #	February 2010	July 2010
	Settlor's wishes as compared to the duty of a fiduciary of an irrevocable trust.	
9	*Negotiable Instruments/ No longer on MEE*	**Corporations** Shareholder voting: importance of "record date" for determining voting eligibility. Proxy agreements: definition and revocability, action inconsistent with a proxy. Shareholder of record may vote at shareholder's meeting. Whether a corporation has the right to vote treasury shares. Whether certificate of incorporation or by-laws control when there is a conflict.

February 2011 and July 2011

Essay #	February 2011	July 2011
1	**Trusts**	**Secured Transactions**
	Trustee with uncontrolled discretion to distribute income and principal.	Security interest in inventory and equipment including future or after acquired items.
	Discretionary trust: rights of creditors no greater than rights of beneficiary to compel trustee to make payments.	Perfection of a security interest.
	Inheritance rights in trust of adopted grandchild who was adopted after testator's death.	Retention of title by seller of delivered goods until payment is made is ineffective and results in an unperfected security interest in goods rather than the retention of title; seller must file a financing statement or retaining possession of goods to perfect a security interest.
	Where trust instrument creates a future interest in grandchildren: when does the class close.	
	Vested remainder: trust provides that if the remainderman predeceases the life tenant that it shall pass to the child of the remainderman and the remainderman dies with no children; common law compared to UPC.	Priority of liens: competing security interests.
		Agreement that is called a lease may be a security interest: "economic realities" of the transaction where lessee becomes the owner after making all payments.

Essay #	February 2011	July 2011
2	**Evidence** Impeaching witness credibility with a prior inconsistent statement. Extrinsic evidence admissible to impeach credibility between prior out-of-court statement and witness's trial testimony. FRE 801(d)(1)(C): non-hearsay statement of identification. FRE 801(d)(1)(A): a prior inconsistent statement admissible as not hearsay when the statement is made under oath, under penalty of perjury at trial, hearing, proceeding, or deposition. FRE 405(a): admissibility of evidence of good character of a relevant character trait may be introduced by defendant only through reputation or opinion testimony.	**Criminal Law and Procedure** Fourth Amendment: whether constitutional reasonableness of a traffic stop depends on the motivation of the officer. Probable cause to stop vehicle based on minor traffic violation. Search and seizure; evidence found in "plain view." *Miranda* rights: determining when they attach (arrested and being questioned). Whether *Miranda* violation's taint's subsequent interrogation. *Miranda* rights: demand for an attorney must be unequivocal and unambiguous as compared to defendant's statement: "Maybe I need a lawyer."

Essay #	February 2011	July 2011
3	**Secured Transactions UCC Article 9** Security interest in inventory. Sale of collateral: no continuation of security interest with a buyer in ordinary course of business (BIOCOB), consumer. Purchase-money security interest in consumer goods and perfected security interest without filing of financing statement; subsequent sale of collateral.	**Trusts** Court's power to reform trust provisions: equitable deviation doctrine; reforming trust terms when there is an unanticipated change in circumstances (expanded under the Uniform Trust Code to include modification of administrative trust provisions as well as dispositive provisions). Bequest to charity that no longer exists, *cy pres* doctrine, presumption of general charitable intent under the UTC.
4	**Torts** Battery: prima facie case, intent to cause a harmful or offensive contact (use of stun gun). Whether frisk as part of routine screening process is "offensive." Defense to battery: consent.	**Real Property** Termination of easement: abandonment, non-use, and intent to abandon. Common law first-in-time, first-in-right principle. Notice-type state recording statute that has a grantor-grantee index.

Essay #	February 2011	July 2011
	Strict products liability: manufacturing defect. "Eggshell skull."	Actual, constructive, or inquiry notice. "Wild deed": deed recorded outside the chain of title and therefore undiscoverable by a reasonable search of the grantor-grantee index; provides no constructive notice to subsequent purchaser. Easement (visible railroad tracks): subsequent purchaser put on inquiry notice.
5	**Family Law** Basis for invalidating a separation agreement's property and support provisions: unconscionability or fraud; whether misrepresentation of paternity would support a finding a fraud. Whether a property division award can be modified after divorce decree is entered.	**Civil Procedure** Determining what is an appealable final judgment. FRCP 54(b): final judgments are immediately appealable when there is "no just reason for delay." Final judgment rule; consideration of the collateral order exception (non-appealable interlocutory order regarding forum-selection clause).

Essay #	February 2011	July 2011
	Modification of spousal-support award and a "substantial change in circumstances." Modification of child-support obligation based on non-paternity.	Whether pendant appellate jurisdiction would apply to allow appellate court to hear appeal where party is seeking review of a non-final order.
6	**Contracts** Offer to modify an existing contract: process of offer, counteroffer, acceptance. Breach of contract: failure to use good faith efforts to obtain loan which was a condition precedent to party's duty to perform. Recovery of expectation damages, including loss of potential investment when foreseeable at time of contract. Punitive damages not recoverable in contract.	**Family Law and Conflict of Laws** Validity of common law marriage in states that do not recognize common law marriages. Requirements to establish a common law marriage. Substantive due process rights under 14th Amendment of unwed biological father. Whether state can permit adoption without the consent of the biological father. Determining a child's "home state" under the Uniform Child Custody Jurisdiction and Enforcement Act to issue

Essay #	February 2011	July 2011
		an initial custody decree (UCCJEA).
7	**Corporations** Filing of articles of incorporation: sets effective date of corporate existence. Liability of persons purporting to act on behalf of corporation with knowledge that articles of incorporation have not been filed. Personal liability by those who purport to act for a corporation if they entered the contract with knowledge there was no incorporation.	*Negotiable Instruments/ No longer on MEE*
8	**Civil Procedure** FRCP 12(b)(6): motion to dismiss for failure to state a cause of action. FRCP 12(b): failure to join other defenses: waiver of defense of insufficient service of process when motion challenging service not	**Constitutional Law** Equal Protection Clause of the Fourteenth Amendment. Gender-based discrimination: separate nursing facilities and programs based on gender. State action doctrine: when can actions of

Essay #	February 2011	July 2011
	joined in initial Rule 12(b) motion.	private party be considered state action.
	FRCP 13(g): defendant's answer may state crossclaim against a co-defendant where the claim arises out of the same transaction or occurrence that is the subject matter of the original action.	Classification based on gender: assessed under heightened or intermediate scrutiny. State must show important governmental objectives and means employed are substantially related to achievement of those objectives.
	Whether federal court has independent subject matter jurisdiction over a state law cross-claim where there is no diversity of citizenship and the amount-in-controversy is not satisfied.	Remedying past discrimination as an "important governmental objective."
	Federal courts' basis for supplemental jurisdiction under 28 U.S.C. § 1367(a) over all claims that "derive from a common nucleus of operative fact."	
9	**Decedents' Estates** Execution requirements of a will: handwritten	**Partnership** Withdrawing from a partnership and

Essay #	February 2011	July 2011
	wills that are properly executed compared to holographic wills.	consequences for the partner and the partnership.
	Whether a life insurance beneficiary be changed by a will provision.	Dissociation when proper and when wrongful.
	Incorporation by reference of memorandum regarding testator's jewelry located in safe deposit box.	Winding-up process: partnership obligations incurred during winding-up period; liability of partners for partnership obligations.
	Lapsed legacy and anti-lapse statute with respect to a husband that predeceases the testator.	
	Abatement of legacies in order of the classification of legacy.	

February 2012 and July 2012

Essay #	February 2012	July 2012
1	**Evidence** FRE 401: relevant evidence. FRE 407: subsequent remedial measures (hospital change in policy). FRE 408: settlement offers of disputed claim. FRE 409: offers to pay medical expenses. FRE 412(a): "Rape Shield" rule. FRE 412(b)(2): in civil cases, otherwise inadmissible evidence of allege victim's sexual behavior is admissible "if its probative value substantially outweighs the danger of harm to any victim."	**Trusts and Future Interests** Irrevocable trust. Termination of trust upon consent of the income beneficiaries and remainder beneficiaries if there is no material purpose yet to be performed. Whether limitation on remarriage of husband beneficiary is a material purpose. Trust remainder to "Settlor's children": gift to a class related to a common ancestor with no condition of survivorship; who qualifies as trust remainder under common law as compared to a jurisdiction that adopted the UPC survivorship statute. "Surviving children" as a class of persons does not close until death of

Essay #	February 2012	July 2012
		"Settlor" and includes children born after the creation of the trust (after-born). Trust termination: trust beneficiaries may direct distribution of trust property in any manner they choose and so direct the trustee.
2	*Negotiable Instruments/ No longer on MEE*	**Criminal Law and Procedure** Involuntary manslaughter: elements. *Mens rea* required for involuntary manslaughter liability; varies by jurisdiction recklessness, gross, criminal, or culpable negligence (defendant dumped bags of marbles at traffic intersection at night resulting in car accident and passenger death). Causation: causation in fact (but for cause) proximate cause.

Essay #	February 2012	July 2012
		Accomplice liability on charge of involuntary manslaughter: elements. Must have *mens rea* required for underlying offense.
3	**Contracts** Substantial performance; when failure to perform or defective performance amounts to a material breach. Determining when a contract is divisible to allow some measure of recovery in event of breach; when a party may be entitled to restitution based on part performance.	**Constitutional Law** Interstate Commerce Clause: Congressional authority to regulate economic activities that have a "substantial economic effect" on interstate commerce (Federal statute against workplace violence). 10th Amendment: federalism, Congress may regulate public and private actors on the same terms. Bar of the 11th Amendment: when abrogation of state immunity is satisfied.
4	**Torts** False imprisonment: elements (refusal to restart a ferris wheel)	**Family Law** Which state has jurisdiction to issue a child custody decree when the child has no "home state":

Essay #	February 2012	July 2012
	Vicarious liability of employer for acts of employee. Negligence: standard of care. Whether parent can bring claim for emotional distress: "zone of danger"; contemporaneously observe injury to child.	pursuant to the Uniform Child Custody Jurisdiction and Enforcement Act, state may exercise jurisdiction based on "significant connections" and "substantial evidence" (UCCJEA). Weight given to older child's wishes or preferences in determining custody: relevant but not determinative. Interpreting a state grandparent child-custody statute: violation of due process of parent when no deference is given to fit parent's determination of best interests of child.
5	**Decedents' Estates** Execution requirements of will. Codicil: cannot republish a will that has not been properly executed; codicil will act as a valid partial will. Incorporation by reference where testator	**Secured Transactions** Perfection of a security interest: present and future inventory, equipment not included. Sale of collateral: no continuation of security interest with a buyer in ordinary course of business (BIOCOB), consumer.

Essay #	February 2012	July 2012
	says "I republish my will": specific identification to the earlier document and testator's intent to incorporate the document. Intestacy distribution rules: "slayer statute" where heir murdered another but did not kill testator. Rule of ademption: specific bequest of real property no longer in testator's estate at time of death; common law ademption compared to "intent test" regarding substitute or replacement property. Effect of a stock dividend or stock split on a specific bequest of "my 400 shares."	Security interest extending beyond inventory to equipment when inventory is traded for equipment. Retention of title by seller of delivered goods until payment is made is ineffective and results in an unperfected security interest in goods rather than the retention of title; seller must file a financing statement or retain possession of goods to perfect a security interest. Priority of liens: competing security interests and a judgment lien.
6	**Partnership** LLP liability for pre-existing judgement against same entity prior	**Torts** Negligence: duty of care owed by university to its students; causation (failure to repair broken lock).

Essay #	February 2012	July 2012
	to its qualification as an LLP. LLP status: partners' liability for partnership obligations incurred prior to qualification as LLP and those incurred after such qualification. Incoming partner's personal liability for LLP's obligations incurred before becoming a partner.	No general duty to come to aid of another: exception if increase in harm and reliance on actor. Duty of psychotherapist: to warn a reasonably identifiable individual of credible threat from patient; no duty to an indeterminate class. "Eggshell skull."
7	**Civil Procedure and Conflict of Laws** When removal from state court to federal court is proper under 28 U.S.C. § 1441(a). Venue: change of venue under 28 U.S.C. § 1404(a) permitted to a court where the action could have been brought originally, convenience of the parties, and "interest of justice." Application of *Erie* Rule following a change of venue: court to which	**Civil Procedure** FRCP 15(a)(2): leave to amend its answer based on facts learned in discovery where defendant previously failed to raise the affirmative defense. Defendant's burden to plead affirmative defenses under FRCP 8(c). FRCP 56(a): standard for grant of summary judgment: "no genuine issue as to any material fact"; in considering the evidence, inferences must be drawn most favorable

Essay #	February 2012	July 2012
	the case is transferred must apply the same law as would have been applied by the original court: change of venue does not affect the law to be applied.	to the party opposing the motion.
8	**Real Property** Appurtenant easement extinguished by merger with a subsequent deed. Creation of easement by implication (implied from prior use): identify criteria. Distribution of proceeds in foreclosure sale with multiple lenders when the first loan which was recorded is a construction loan or "future-advance" mortgage. Whether future-advances mortgage payments are required or optional determines the rights of junior lender.	**Corporations and LLCs** Member-managed LLC; whether majority member of member-managed LLC has fiduciary duties that require it to bring claims against an LLC member. Claim of LLC v. claim of individual member of LLC. When a derivative action in a member-managed LLC may be brought. Involuntary dissolution: "oppression doctrine" as applied to LLC. Limited liability of LLC members and managers: piercing the LLC veil.

Essay #	February 2012	July 2012
9	**Corporations** Notice requirements for special meeting of directors (stating the purpose of meeting not necessary): waiver of notice by a director by attending and voting. Quorum required for action at special meeting of board of directors. What it means to be "legally present" at a meeting: all directors must be able to simultaneously hear all others who are present.	**Decedents' Estates and Conflict of Laws** Conflict of laws: domicile and distribution of personal property, real property and law of the situs. Holographic wills and interpretation of two different state statutes with different execution requirements where both statutes find the will invalid—all assets to pass intestate. Interpretation of two different state intestacy statutes with regard to inheritance rights of biological, adopted, and non-marital child when paternity has been established; constitutional standards.

February 2013 and July 2013

Essay #	February 2013	July 2013
1	**Real Property**	**Civil Procedure**
	Landlord/tenant: commercial lease with term-of-years.	Jurisdiction: federal subject matter jurisdiction based on diversity of citizenship (28 U.S.C. § 1332(a)).
	Constructive eviction: elements at common law.	Determining domicile: residence and "intent to remain."
	No implied duty for landlord to repair leased premises under common law; courts reluctant to imply duty to repair in commercial leases.	Determining citizenship for corporations: dual citizenship based on state where incorporated and where corp. has its principal place of business ("nerve center" test).
	Written lease contained no term requiring landlord to repair the air-conditioning.	Venue: basis for venue when jurisdiction is based on diversity (28 U.S.C. § 1391(b)).
	Covenant of quiet enjoyment does not include duty to repair.	Obtaining personal jurisdiction over a corporate defendant (FRCP 4(k)).
	Surrender of a lease by tenant and whether the landlord accepted the surrender (retaining keys) or held the tenant to lease terms.	Exercise of state's long-arm statute where it extends jurisdiction as far as Due Process Clause of

Essay #	February 2013	July 2013
	Common law rule: landlord had not duty to mitigate damages and not entitled to recover unpaid future rents, only what was in arrears at time of suit. Other courts allow landlords to sue tenants for wrongful termination and seek damages equal to difference between unpaid rent due and fair market rental value or other valuations for unpaid future rent.	the 14th Amendment allows.
2	**Contracts/Article 2** UCC Article 2 sale of goods. Reasonable grounds for insecurity regarding prospective performance; written demand for adequate assurances; when failure to provide such assurances constitute a repudiation. Retracting a repudiation.	**Torts** Vicarious liability of employer for acts of employee committed within the scope of employment. Principal's liability for agent's torts based on apparent authority of employee. Negligence: causation.

Essay #	February 2013	July 2013
3	**Constitutional Law** First Amendment: freedom of speech (refusal to recite pledge of allegiance). State action where private actor exercises a "public function (running a privately owned "company town"). First Amendment ban on compelled expression; compelled expression of a political belief (school required students to salute flag and Pledge Allegiance). Regulation of student speech by schools and teachers. Traditional public forum: content-neutral regulation of speech, intermediate scrutiny of a statute (preventing leaflet distribution).	**Family Law** Whether a court would order a parent to stop making contributions from her earnings to a religious organization. Court intervention in parental disputes: whether a court would require one parent to follow the other's preference with respect to child rearing practices (allowing daughter to take skating lessons). Court intervention when health or safety of child is at issue because of parent's religious belief; court may order medication given to child. Whether court may deny a parent custody based the parent's religious faith based on a threat to the child's health or safety: "best interests of the child."

Essay #	February 2013	July 2013
4	**UCC Article 9** Perfection of a security interest: "purchase-money security interest" in consumer goods without a financing statement. Sale of collateral and continuation of security interest with a buyer who is not a buyer in the ordinary course of business (BIOCOB), but rather is a buyer of goods used for "personal, family or household purposes." Gift of collateral, for no value and the continuation of a security interest.	**Evidence** Hearsay; exceptions to hearsay (911 call). FRE 803 (1): present sense impressions. FRE 803 (2): "excited utterances." FRE 803 (4): "statements made for medical diagnosis and treatment." Sixth Amendment Confrontation Clause: whether the statement to police was testimonial.
5	**Civil Procedure** Claim preclusion (*res judicata*): determining issues of privity between parties (family relationship). Issue preclusion (*collateral estoppel*):	*Negotiable Instruments/* *No longer on MEE*

Essay #	February 2013	July 2013
	effect of privity on non-party's ability to present her claim in a second suit even if it is factually related to claims and defenses presented in first suit. Non-mutual issue preclusion: abandonment of "traditional" requirement of mutuality where the party asserting issue preclusion and party against whom it was asserted were both bound by the prior judgment.	
6	**Agency** Defining the agency relationship. Power of agent to bind principal. Actual and apparent authority. Agent exceeding authority or acting without authority and consequences.	**Corporations and LLCs** Member-managed LLC: members in a fiduciary relationship with duty of utmost trust and loyalty. Where member participates in a competing business but the express terms of the operating agreement allow members to have such an interest ("opting-out" of the duty of loyalty).

Essay #	February 2013	July 2013
	Types of authority: actual, inherent, and apparent authority. Undisclosed, partially disclosed, and unidentified principals: impact on liability for contracts entered into by agent. Effect of ratification on contract by undisclosed principal: whether owner is liable depends on whether court follows Second or Third Restatement of Agency.	Liability of members for debts of LLC: improper dissolution and winding up of LLC; notice to creditors. Piercing the LLC veil: "alter ego" where factors are considered: improper use of the LLC form, siphoning funds, intermingling personal and business funds, failure to follow corporate accounting formalities.
7	**Evidence** FRE 401: relevant evidence. Hearsay: text message is a "written assertion." FRE 803(1): hearsay exception for present sense impressions. FRE 803(6): text message as a business record. "Thumbs-up" as a non-verbal assertion made	**Contracts/Article 2** UCC Article 2 sale of goods. Statute of frauds: sale of goods over $500. Application of "merchant confirmatory memo" exception. What constitutes a signature to satisfy the statute of frauds. Where statute of frauds is not satisfied but the

Essay #	February 2013	July 2013
	out-of-court: when hearsay and when not.	contract is valid in other respects, it is enforceable as to the goods which have received and accepted.
8	**Trusts and Future Interests** Revocable trust (inter vivos); whether a revocable trust is amendable. Settlor's power of revocation includes the power to amend trust when trust is silent on power to amend or modify. Settlor's ability to amend trust without formalities necessary to execute a will (no need for witnesses to Settlor's signature). Revocable trust may be amended any time prior to Settlor's death and the amendment applies to assets conveyed to the trust in a pour-over will where the will was	**Real Property** New home construction: implied warranty against latent defects, implied warranty of fitness, implied warranty of habitability (rejection of caveat emptor doctrine). Extension of implied warranty of latent defects to remote grantees or subsequent purchasers in most jurisdictions (despite lack of privity with builder). Assumption of mortgage: express assumption required for personal liability on unpaid mortgage obligation; implied assumption of mortgage. Quitclaim deeds: contain no warranties of title.

Essay #	February 2013	July 2013
	executed prior to amendment. Rule Against Perpetuities: interpreting the state statute provided in the MEE question; applying common law rule to determine validity of Settlor's trust.	
9	*Negotiable Instruments/* *No longer on MEE*	**Decedents' Estates** Prenuptial agreement: waiving rights in spouse's estate will not preclude a surviving spouse from inheriting from a will that was executed after the prenuptial agreement was signed. Divorce: when parties have only filed for divorce as compared to a final divorce at the time of the testator's death. Adopted-out child: rights to inherit when child is adopted out by a family member.

Essay #	February 2013	July 2013
		Appointment of personal representative when will is silent; priority of devisees.

February 2014 and July 2014

Essay #	February 2014	July 2014
1	**Constitutional Law** Fifth Amendment: city ordinance requiring business to install floodlights is not a *per se* taking. Unconstitutional regulatory taking of property without unjust compensation compared to regulating with a legitimate state interest. Determining a regulatory taking: three-part balancing test under *Penn Central*. Exaction of an easement to obtain a building permit, uncompensated taking, *Dolan* test.	**Criminal Law and Procedure** Sixth Amendment right to counsel: is charge—or offense—specific; does not attach to uncharged crimes where there is no formal adversarial judicial proceeding. *Miranda* rights: demand for an attorney must be unequivocal and unambiguous as compared to defendant's statement: "I think I want my lawyer here before I talk to you." *Miranda* rights: standard for waiver of rights is voluntary, knowing, and intelligent.
2	**Trusts and Future Interests** Testamentary trust. Determining what constitutes income and principal, sale of proceeds of real estate, rental proceeds, cash	**Contracts** Consideration: modification and pre-existing duty rule. Exception under the Restatement (Second) for changed circumstances that were unanticipated at

Essay #	February 2014	July 2014
	dividends, and stock dividends. Disclaimer made more than 9 months after testator's death is invalid pursuant to state statute; income beneficiary who invalidly disclaims is not deemed to have predeceased testator; common law rule allowing disclaimers at any time; acceleration of remainder not available where the remainder in will has survivorship contingency.	the time of contract and the modification would be fair and equitable. UCC Article 2: consideration not required for modifications made in good faith. Defense of economic duress/business compulsion: when a threat of non-performance is "wrongful" or "improper."
3	**UCC Article 9** Security interest in equipment including future or after acquired items. Priority of liens: competing security interests and "first to file-or-perfect rule." Filing financing statement before security agreement or loan is obtained,	**Family Law** Interstate enforcement and modification of child support orders (UIFSA), personal jurisdiction, subject matter jurisdiction, enforcement in non-issuing state. UIFSA: does not govern property distributions in divorce decree. Modification of child support obligation,

Essay #	February 2014	July 2014
	attachment, and determining the date of perfection. Sale of collateral and continuation of security interest in equipment where buyer is not a buyer in ordinary course of business (BIOCOB) because seller is not in the business of selling goods of that kind.	retroactive modification, prospective support obligation and "substantial change in circumstances", involuntary loss of income or voluntary loss of income. Modification of property-division award in divorce decree, personal jurisdiction and property division.
4	**Civil Procedure** FRCP 26(b)(1), FRCP 34(a)(1). Discovery: work product rule: whether a document prepared in the course of a contract dispute is non-discoverable "work product" when the document was not prepared in anticipation of litigation. Discovery; destruction of discoverable materials, deletion of potentially relevant emails when litigation is possible, role	**Civil Procedure** FRCP 24(a): intervention as a matter of right; identification of the three requirements for intervention of right. Standard and requirements for granting TRO under FRCP 65(b). Standard for granting preliminary injunction: (1) risk of "irreparable harm" to plaintiff if preliminary injunction is not granted; (2) likelihood of plaintiff's success on the merits of the underlying claim; (3) "balance of the equities"–

Essay #	February 2014	July 2014
	of routine document retention/destruction policy. Duty to preserve discoverable materials when litigation is anticipated. Determining appropriate sanctions for spoliation of evidence: court considers the level of culpability of the spoliating party and the degree of prejudice the loss of evidence causes the other party.	likelihood that the harm the plaintiff will suffer in the absence of the preliminary injunction outweighs the harm the defendant will suffer if it is granted; (4) the public interest.
5	**Criminal Law and Procedure** Fifth Amendment: double jeopardy, two crimes with different elements, theft and burglary. Due Process Clause requires the prosecution to prove all elements of offense beyond a reasonable doubt: jury instructions which create either an "irrebutable conclusive presumption"	**Evidence** Impeachment of witnesses with evidence of prior convictions and specific instances of misconduct (felony drug conviction, perjury, sexual assault). FRE 609(a): evidence of prior convictions admissible to attack witness's character for truthfulness. FRE 609(b): determining the 10-year time limit for

Essay #	February 2014	July 2014
	or a "rebuttable presumption" unconstitutionally shift burden of proof to the defendant. Sixth Amendment: right to jury trial on element of offense, where the value of stolen goods may increase the penalty for a crime, said value is a question for the jury and must be proved beyond a reasonable doubt.	admissibility: limit runs from date of conviction or release from confinement whichever is later. Admissibility of evidence subject to FRE 403 balancing test. FRE 608(b): cross-examination of witness about specific instance of prior non-conviction misconduct (lying on job application and resume). FRE 608(b): forbids use of extrinsic evidence to impeach witness's character for truthfulness.
6	**Agency and Partnership** Partner liability in general partnership: joint and several liability for misrepresentations made by partner in the ordinary course of the partnership business. Extent of personal liability of incoming partner in a general partnership on existing	**Corporations** Whether shareholders have authority to amend corporation's bylaws and if so, what are proper matters (e.g., procedures for nominating directors). Shareholders' power to amend or repeal board-approved bylaws. Derivative suit: to vindicate corporate rights;

Essay #	February 2014	July 2014
	claims against the partnership. How a general partnership can make an election and become a limited liability partnership. After the filing by a general partnership of a statement of qualification as a limited liability partnership, whether the partners are personally liable as partners on (a) an existing claim against the general partnership and (b) a claim against the partnership that arose after the filing.	must make demand on the board. Ability of shareholders to bring direct suit: to vindicate shareholder's own rights.

February 2015 and July 2015

Essay #	February 2015	July 2015
1	**Torts** Independent contractor vs. employee Vicarious liability of employer for acts of employee committed within the scope of employment. Negligence *per se:* violation of traffic ordinance (double-parking). Whether conforming to custom is a defense to negligence. Indemnification of employer by employee for tort claim.	**Torts** Negligence: minor engaged in a hazardous, adult activity (snowmobiling). Standard of care owed by landowner to a trespasser and to a licensee. Attractive nuisance doctrine. No general duty to come to aid of another: exception if increase in harm and reliance on actor. Contributory/comparative negligence.
2	**Constitutional Law** Age-based discrimination. Equal Protection Clause of the Fourteenth Amendment: three levels of scrutiny for EP claims. Scope of congressional authority under Section	**Civil Procedure** FRCP (4)(k)(1)(A): asserting personal jurisdiction over a non-resident defendant. Exercise of state's long-arm statute where it extends jurisdiction as far as the Due Process Clause of the 14th Amendment

Essay #	February 2015	July 2015
	Five of Fourteenth Amendment.	allows; evaluation of contacts with a forum state.
		Jurisdiction: 28 U.S.C. § 1331: original jurisdiction, cause of action based on violating a federal statute.
		Jurisdiction: 28 U.S.C. § 1367: supplemental jurisdiction, "same case or controversy" even though based on contract claim or state claim.
3	**Secured Transactions UCC Article 9** Criteria for a valid security interest. Security interest in "accounts" and "inventory." Classifying property as an account, inventory, or equipment. Inventory: raw materials as inventory, items left for repair by customers are not inventory.	**Contracts/Article 2** Statute of frauds: sale of goods over $500, oral agreement followed by a signed letter indicating that the contract exists. Repudiation of contract, attempted retraction of repudiation. Damages: difference between contract price and resale price plus incidental damages.

Essay #	February 2015	July 2015
	Sale of collateral: no continuation of security interest with a buyer in ordinary course of business (BIOCOB), consumer to consumer. Priority of liens: competing security interest and a judgment lien.	
4	**Real Property** Adverse possession: elements, calculating the 10-year statutory period by tacking of time of previous possessors. Title acquired by adverse possession extends to only occupied portion and not entire parcel of land. Warranty deed: 6 covenants, present and future covenants, breach of covenant of seisin. Easement: buyer taking property subject to existing sewer-line easement.	**Corporations** Director's conflicting interest transaction/director self-dealing. Business judgment rule. Safe harbor for director who breaches his duty of loyalty: approval by disinterested directors, approval by disinterested shareholders, or fairness (RMBCA). Corporate directors' breach of duty of loyalty where unable to show that the transaction was fair to the corporation even if not properly authorized.

Essay #	February 2015	July 2015
		Corporate directors' breach of duty of care by failure to be adequately informed prior to decision-making.
5	**Civil Procedure** FRCP 4 (h): service of process on a corporation. Subject matter jurisdiction based on federal question (sexual harassment and sex discrimination claim). Subject matter jurisdiction over third party complaint for state law claim, breach of contract: based on diversity, Determining corporate citizenship for purposes of diversity. Determining domicile and amount-in-controversy requirement. FRCP 14(a): impleader rules, improper joinder of claims, third-party	**Criminal Law and Procedure** Affirmative defense: requirements to establish defense of not guilty by reason of insanity (NGRI). Manslaughter: elements; *actus reus and mens rea* (death caused by the criminal operation of a motor vehicle). Affirmative defense: duress (knife held to throat of the defendant).

Essay #	February 2015	July 2015
	claim based on derivative liability.	
6	**Decedents' Estates** Revocation of will or a portion of a will: testamentary intention to revoke and physical act; writing on will to "call lawyer to fix" is only intent to have will reviewed, not revoked. Rights of after-born child (pretermitted child) not mentioned in will. Distribution of assets of revocable trust: interpreting state intestacy statute and state statute regarding "illusory" revocable trusts (created during marriage).	**Trusts** Testamentary trust. Provision of trust that violates public policy is void (condition of marriage). Duty of loyalty: self-dealing, trustee purchasing stock from trust; trust beneficiaries may seek to rescission of the transaction or seek damages. Duty to invest trust assets in a prudent manner (mutual funds decline in value during economic downturn).

February 2016 and July 2016

Essay #	February 2016	July 2016
1	**Secured Transactions UCC Article 9** Security interest in "present and future inventory" in a store; buyer in ordinary course of business (BIOCOB) and "shelter principle" affecting subsequent transfers. Perfection of retailer's security interest: "purchase-money security interest" in "consumer goods"; retailer retaining title is in effect a security interest. Sale of collateral: no continuation of security interest with a buyer in ordinary course of business (BIOCOB), consumer to consumer. Security interests in proceeds (check) of sale of collateral.	**Limited Liability Companies** Determining whether an LLC is member-managed or manager-managed when its certificate of organization and operating agreement is silent. Whether a member in a member-managed LLC had actual or apparent authority to bind the LLC to a contract based on determinations of whether the acts were within the ordinary course of the LLC's activities or outside it. Consequences of an LLC member's withdrawal: constitutes a "dissociation" and not a "dissolution" and winding up of the business.

Essay #	February 2016	July 2016
2	**Evidence** Hearsay; exceptions to hearsay. FRE 803 (1): present sense impressions. FRE 803 (2): "excited utterances." Sixth Amendment Confrontation Clause: whether the statement was testimonial (arguments either way in this case). FRE 801(d)(1)(C): admissibility of out-of-court statement of identification testified to at trial. Character evidence: inadmissible to show propensity.	**Evidence and Criminal Procedure** *Miranda* rights: whether defendant's crying is a testimonial communication. Hearsay; exceptions to hearsay, non-hearsay. FRE 803(5): recorded recollections. FRE 801(d)(2): non-hearsay (statement of opposing party). FRE 803(5): even if written notes meet exception to be read into evidence, admissible as an exhibit only if offered by the adverse party. Whether post-invocation statements are admissible when custodial suspect initiates communication with police: fresh set of Miranda warnings required. Police obligation to honor an invocation of *Miranda* right to counsel terminates 14 days after suspect has

Essay #	February 2016	July 2016
		been released from interrogative custody (*Maryland v. Shatzer*).
3	**Agency and Partnership** LLP's liability based on LLP partner's apparent authority to take out a bank loan. LLP partner's limited liability for partnership debts; exception for personal misconduct. Partners' fiduciary duties to the partnership and other partners: duty of loyalty, duty of care. Partners' liability for damages to the partnership and co-partners for breach. Partnership and individually injured partner can bring a direct action against the breaching partner and an accounting action.	**Torts** Medical malpractice: standard of care for the relevant specialty and medical community. Negligence. Strict products liability (pesticide in herbal tea); manufacturing defect. Implied warranty of merchantability. Causation requirement not met where multiple product manufacturers and plaintiff cannot link any particular defendant to his injury. Strict products liability claim against commercial seller.
4	**Constitutional Law** Commerce Clause: state statute that applies	**Secured Transactions and Real Property** **UCC Article 9**

Essay #	February 2016	July 2016
	equally to in-state and out-of-state utilities. Where a state statute treats in-state electricity consumers more favorably than out-of-state consumers. Where state acts as a "market participant."	Remedies available to a secured creditor when debtor defaults on "equipment"; whether "self-help" is available. Security interest in equipment: defining "equipment" under Article 9. Perfection of a security interest in equipment including fixtures. Determining the priority of interests in equipment after it becomes a fixture when a bank holds a mortgage on the real property; exception relating to the priority of a "purchase-money security interest" in fixtures as against an encumbrance of the related real property. "Fixture filing."
5	**Decedents' Estates** Agent's authority to act under a durable health-care power of attorney (POA).	**Contracts** Whether contract rights may be assigned without the obligor's consent when the assignment does not

Essay #	February 2016	July 2016
	Protection of agent from civil (wrongful death action) and criminal liability when acting in good faith. "Slayer statute": where one who intentionally caused the decedent's death is barred from sharing in the estate with regard to health care POA.	change the obligor's duty in any material respect. What is required for an effective assignment. The assignee's rights to enforce the contract when the obligor does not perform. Determining third-party beneficiary status: differences between incidental vs. intended beneficiaries. Delegation of duties: where obligor remains liable for any breach by the delegate.
6	**Family Law** Determining enforceability of premarital agreement under the Uniform Premarital Agreement Act (UPAA): voluntariness, unconscionability, reasonable disclosure of assets and liabilities.	**Civil Procedure** FRCP 4(k)(1)(A): transient jurisdiction: personal jurisdiction based on service of process of defendant who is physically present in the state. Jurisdiction: 28 U.S.C. § 1331: subject matter jurisdiction; federal

Essay #	February 2016	July 2016
	Determination of marital property and separate property; principles of equitable distribution; winning lottery ticket purchased before divorce filing.	question jurisdiction based on a federal statute. Jurisdiction: diversity jurisdiction (lack of diversity) 28 U.S.C. § 1332 over state-law negligence claim. Jurisdiction: 28 U.S.C. § 1367: supplemental jurisdiction, "same case or controversy" over a negligence or state claim. Venue: Determining appropriate venue under 28 U.S.C. § 1391(b).

February 2017 and July 2017

Essay #	February 2017	July 2017
1	**Contracts/Article 2** Offer formation under the Code; whether a party is a merchant. Irrevocable offers; "firm offers." Output contracts.	**Torts** Strict products liability: whether public fireworks display is an abnormally dangerous activity. Negligence; negligence *per se.* Burden of taking precautions compared to risk of harm. Assessing proximate cause: danger invites rescue. Vicarious liability: whether one who employs an independent contractor is liable for harm caused by the independent contractor when the contractor is hired to engage in work involving a special danger to others and the employer knows about such danger.
2	**Trusts** Revocable trust. Settlor's power of revocation includes the	**Constitutional Law** State's sovereign immunity under the 11th Amendment

Essay #	February 2017	July 2017
	power to amend trust when trust is silent on power to amend or modify. Under UTC, power to revoke or amend is exercisable by will unless the trust instrument provides otherwise. Power of appointment (specific not general) created in Settlor's trust and exercised in a subsequent will; "permissible appointees" compared to "impermissible appointees." Taker in default of ineffective appointment. Right of election. Surviving spouse's right to the elective share of probate assets pursuant to a state statute. Illusory transfer doctrine and fraudulent transfer doctrine (available in some jurisdictions) allowing surviving spouse	from suit for damages in federal court. *Ex parte Young*: suit against State's Superintendent of Banking to enjoin enforcement of allegedly unconstitutional statute not barred by 11th Amendment when it is an official-capacity action and seeks prospective relief. Dormant commerce clause: balancing test is used when the state law is nondiscriminatory on its face (because it applies equally to local and out-of-state banks) but still imposes an incidental burden on interstate commerce.

Essay #	February 2017	July 2017
	to exercise the right of election to claim trust assets held in a revocable trust.	
3	**Family Law and Conflict of Laws** Requirements to establish a common law marriage. Recognition of common law marriage in other states. Determination of marital property; principles of equitable distribution. Putative-spouse doctrine. Illegality of bigamy: when a first marriage is not legally dissolved, a second marriage has no legal effect. Presumption that the latest in a series of marriages is valid: designed to protect parties' expectations but may be rebutted. Property and support rights between	**Secured Transactions** Perfection of a security interest in "present and future accounts." UCC Article 9 criteria for attachment of a security interest. Priority of liens: competing security interests and "first to file or perfect rule." Determining priority of interests between perfected and unperfected interests. Discharge of obligations by account debtors to assignee upon receiving notice of the assignment.

Essay #	February 2017	July 2017
	unmarried co-habitants based on an express or implied contract to share assets. Fundamental right of parents to control the upbringing of their children; a fit parent is presumed to act in the best interests of her children. Determining non-parent's visitation rights.	
4	**Corporations** Shareholder's right to inspect accounting records and board minutes if there is a "proper purpose"; proper purpose as a shareholder includes trying to determine whether improper corporate transactions have occurred. Shareholder has burden to show credible evidence of possible mismanagement to	**Decedent's Estates/ Future Interests** Execution requirements of will. Validity of will when witnessed by an interested witness and effect on the bequest to that witness. Codicil: republication-by-codicil doctrine cures defect in previously validly executed will with interested witness problem. Bequest of household goods (furniture) made in

Essay #	February 2017	July 2017
	obtain inspection of books and records. When the board can seek dismissal of a shareholder's derivative suit: need for good faith, reasonable inquiry by majority of board's qualified directors into the shareholder's allegations. Fiduciary and good faith duties of directors; when the business judgment rule protects directors' conduct.	an unattested document (memo) written after the will was executed and the will evidences intent to so dispose of the property. Whether a bequest violates the Rule Against Perpetuities (RAP). Vesting of a class gift for purposes of the RAP when the class is closed and all members of the class have met any conditions precedent.
5	**Agency** Defining the agency relationship. Agents: scope of authority; actual, inherent, and apparent authority. Power of agent to bind the principal: • Liability to third party when agent enters into a contract with a	**Evidence/Criminal Law and Procedure** Relevant evidence. Hearsay, non-hearsay, & exceptions to hearsay. Hearsay: when an out-of-court statement is not hearsay. Whether criminal defendant's admission violates *Miranda* when the police officer's question was limited to weapons

Essay #	February 2017	July 2017
	third party on behalf of a disclosed principal on terms not authorized by the principal. • Liability to third party when agent enters into a contract with a third party on behalf of an undisclosed principal on terms authorized by the principal but the principal later repudiates the contract. • Liability to third party when agent enters into a contract on behalf of a partially disclosed principal for goods different from those authorized by the principal and the principal accepts the goods.	and asked after a shooting (public safety exception to *Miranda*). Non-hearsay: statement of opposing party Hearsay exceptions: custodian describing what he heard around the time of the incident: • FRE 803 (1): hearsay exception: present sense impressions; or • FRE 803 (2): "excited utterances."

Essay #	February 2017	July 2017
6	**Real Property** Landlord/tenant. Validity of lease provision requiring landlord's written consent for assignment; whether refusal to consent to assignment must be reasonable. Actions constituting an abandonment of the premises. Landlord's options when tenant abandons: accept surrender of the premises; re-let or attempt to re-let the premises and leave the premises vacant and sue tenant for unpaid rent. Landlord's duty to mitigate.	**Civil Procedure and Conflict of Laws** FRCP 12—whether a motion to dismiss can be amended prior to a responsive filing (no prejudice or delay to other party) to add a ground for dismissal that would have been waived because it was not raised in the initial Rule 12(b)(6) motion to dismiss. FRCP 4(e): insufficient service of process when documents are not personally served but delivered to parents' home where defendant used to live. Choice-of-law rules: a federal court sitting in diversity applies the choice-of-law rules of the state where the federal court sits (Restatement) and according to a signed contract between the parties.

February 2018 and July 2018

Essay #	February 2018	July 2018
1	**Family Law** Enforceability of premarital agreement with property division, alimony, and child custody provisions. Divisibility of marital assets at divorce: separate and marital property. Whether a parent's adulterous conduct is considered by the court in making a custody decision. "Best interests of the child": factors in determining child custody.	**Constitutional Law** Whether a federal act requiring state officers/agencies to assist in the enforcement of federal drug laws violates fundamental principles of federalism. Concepts of federalism and dual sovereignty. Constitutional exercise of Congress's spending power when it conditions the granting of federal funds on a state's compliance with "federal statutory and administrative directives.
2	**Criminal Law** Determining whether a criminal defendant is competent to stand trial. If found competent and the prosecution proceeds, whether a jurisdiction that follows the *M'Naughten* test	**Contracts/Article 2** Determining whether UCC Article 2 applies to a transaction involving a lawnmower. Offer; rejection; renewing an offer.

Essay #	February 2018	July 2018
	should find the defendant not guilty by reason of insanity (NGRI).	Promise to keep an offer open: by common law, by statute, by reliance. Terminating the power of acceptance: indirect revocation.
3	**Contracts/Article 2** Determining whether UCC Article 2 or the common law applies under a mixed contract: predominant purpose test. Applicability of the parol evidence rule to a prior oral agreement. Consideration: modification and pre-existing duty rule.	**Real Property** Application of the nonconforming-use doctrine: whether proposed changes to expand a convenience store are exempt from the zoning ordinance as a nonconforming use depends on whether they are substantial or unsubstantial changes. "Future-advances" loan: whether the bank's commitment to make future advances optional or obligatory. Determining whether a bank's mortgage has priority over a mechanic's lien when the mortgage was recorded and payment was made before the filing of the lien.

Essay #	February 2018	July 2018
4	**Real Property** Whether there was a breach of a warranty deed's title covenants, specifically, the covenant against encumbrances. Whether damages are available for breach of the covenant against encumbrances when the easement was plain and obvious and if so, what they would be. Whether there was a breach of the implied warranty of habitability.	**Trusts and Future Interests** Duties of trustee to the trust beneficiaries. Duty of loyalty: trustee rented a trust-owned apartment to himself but paid the market rate (self-dealing); "no-further-inquiry rule." Duty of prudent administration (duty of care): trustee failed to purchase fire/casualty insurance on the trust's real property. Duty to comply with applicable law: trustee allocated a $50,000 repair expense necessitated by a fire exclusively to income when it should have been allocated to principal. Distribution of trust principal where the remainder interest was vested.

Essay #	February 2018	July 2018
5	**Civil Procedure** FRCP 11: filing an answer with a general denial of factual and legal contentions where the attorney made no inquiry into the facts before doing so. Procedure for presenting a Rule 11 motion: giving attorney an opportunity to correct the pleading. Court's discretion in imposing sanctions; possible sanctions; on whom sanctions may be imposed: the party, the attorney the law firm.	**Evidence** Admissibility of relevant evidence. Opinion evidence: lay and expert opinion. Hearsay; business-records exception. Physician-patient privilege; patient's waiver of the privilege by filing a civil lawsuit placing her medical condition "in issue." Non-hearsay: statement by an opposing party. Hearsay exception for statements made for medical diagnosis or treatment. Question of whether roommate's texting behavior is evidence of habit or character.
6	**Partnership** Partner's right to dissolve an at-will partnership. Partner's continuing duties to the partnership during the winding-up process.	**Corporations and LLCs** Determining when a corporation comes into existence: filing of articles of incorporation. Personal liability on a contract by a party acting

Essay #	February 2018	July 2018
	Partner's fiduciary duties to the partnership and other parties during the winding-up process; duty not to appropriate partnership opportunities during the winding-up of the partnership business.	on behalf of a corporation when she did not know that the business had not been properly incorporated. Limited liability in cases of defective incorporation: "de facto corporation" and "corporation by estoppel" doctrine. Personal liability of inactive investor in the business on an employment contract; apply defective-incorporation principles, de facto corporation, and corporation by estoppel doctrines.

2018 Subject Charts

Business Associations: Agency and Partnership

Exam Date & Question	Business Associations: Agency and Partnership
Feb. 2005 Essay 7	**Agency** Defining the agency relationship. Undisclosed principals and liability of undisclosed principal for contracts (purchase of supplies and employment contract) entered into by general agent in violation of principal's instructions. Types of authority: actual, inherent, and apparent authority.
Feb. 2006 Essay 2	**Agency** Vicarious liability of employer for acts of employees committed within the scope of employment. Defining the agency relationship: reflected in master-servant relationship. Factors distinguishing between independent contractor and employer/employee. Fiduciary duties of agent/employee: duty to obey reasonable instructions and duty to act solely for benefit of principal.
July 2006 Essay 2	**Agency and Partnership** Definition of partnership: determining whether parties are partners based on a loan to the partnership (no) but forgiveness of the loan in exchange of share of the profits (yes). Partner as agent of partnership: partner's authority to bind partnership for an act for

Exam Date & Question	Business Associations: Agency and Partnership
	carrying on the ordinary course of partnership business, but not for an act outside the ordinary business. Actual and apparent authority. Partners' joint and several liability for partnership obligations.
Feb. 2007 Essay 6	**Agency and Partnership** Limited partnership. Right of limited partners to obtain information from general partner regarding the financial condition of the business upon "reasonable demand": tax returns, contracts, correspondence. Liability of limited partners in a limited liability partnership: generally not liable for the obligations of a limited partnership unless participate in the "control of the business." "Safe harbor": RULPA's list of activities that do not constitute the exercise of control of the business includes removal of a general partner. Participation in control of business can make limited partners liable for obligations of limited partnership under certain circumstances.
July 2007 Essay 4	**Agency and Partnership** Definition of partnership: intent to form a partnership; written agreement not required. Partner as agent of partnership: partner's authority to bind partnership for an act for carrying on the ordinary course of partnership

Exam Date & Question	Business Associations: Agency and Partnership
	business; acts outside the ordinary course of business require consent of all partners.
	Actual and apparent authority.
	A partner is jointly and severally liable for partnership obligations; partner liability includes unpaid wages of an employee.
	Personal liability of general partner and limited partners for partnership's debts.
	Procedure for recovering against partners personally: judgment must first be obtained individually against each partner and against the partnership and levy execution against partnership assets.
July 2008 Essay 3	**Agency and Partnership** Identifying partnership property. Whether partnership property is subject to attachment and execution by judgment creditor of individual partner. How creditor of individual partner can collect from a partner's financial interest in a partnership. Assignment of partnership interest: rights of assignee (financial interest only). Types of partnerships: partnership for term, partnership at will, or partnership for a particular undertaking; how type of partnership affects a forced dissolution.

Exam Date & Question	Business Associations: Agency and Partnership
Feb. 2009 **Essay 1**	**Agency** Defining the agency relationship (consulting contract). Power of agent to bind principal (to a contract). Actual and apparent authority. Agent exceeding authority or acting without authority and consequences.
July 2009 **Essay 8**	**Partnership** Determining type of entity: limited partnership or general partnership when no general partner signs the limited partnership agreement. Partner liability for partnership obligations or debt; partners jointly and severally liable. Procedure for recovering against partners personally: judgment must first be obtained individually against each partner and against the partnership and levy execution against partnership assets. Partner liability for tort (wrongful death); joint and several liability.
July 2010 **Essay 1**	**Partnership** Definition of partnership: formation of general partnership. Characteristics of a partner: distinguishing between one who receives share of profits from one who receives payment from profits to pay off a loan.

Exam Date & Question	Business Associations: Agency and Partnership
	Assignment of partnership interest and rights of assignee to receive profits; assignee does not become a partner unless the other partner(s) consent. Identifying partnership property and the misuse of partnership property by a partner.
July 2011 Essay 9	Partnership Withdrawing from a partnership and consequences for the partner and the partnership. Dissociation when proper and when wrongful. Winding-up process: partnership obligations incurred during winding-up period; liability of partners for partnership obligations.
Feb. 2012 Essay 6	Partnership LLP liability for pre-existing judgement against same entity prior to its qualification as an LLP. LLP status: partners' liability for partnership obligations incurred prior to qualification as LLP and those incurred after such qualification. Incoming partner's personal liability for LLP's obligations incurred before becoming a partner.

Exam Date & Question	Business Associations: Agency and Partnership
Feb. 2013 Essay 6	**Agency** Defining the agency relationship. Power of agent to bind principal. Actual and apparent authority. Agent exceeding authority or acting without authority and consequences. Types of authority: actual, inherent, and apparent authority. Undisclosed, partially disclosed, and unidentified principals: impact on liability for contracts entered into by agent. Effect of ratification on contract by undisclosed principal: whether owner is liable depends on whether court follows Second or Third Restatement of Agency.
Feb. 2014 Essay 6	**Agency and Partnership** Partner liability in general partnership: joint and several liability for misrepresentations made by partner in the ordinary course of the partnership business. Extent of personal liability of incoming partner in a general partnership on existing claims against the partnership. How a general partnership can make an election and become a limited liability partnership. After the filing by a general partnership of a statement of qualification as a limited liability partnership, whether the partners are personally liable as partners on (a) an existing claim against

Exam Date & Question	Business Associations: Agency and Partnership
	the general partnership and (b) a claim against the partnership that arose after the filing.
Feb. 2016 Essay 3	**Agency and Partnership** LLP's liability based on LLP partner's apparent authority to take out a bank loan. LLP partner's limited liability for partnership debts; exception for personal misconduct. Partners' fiduciary duties to the partnership and other partners: duty of loyalty, duty of care. Partners' liability for damages to the partnership and co-partners for breach. Partnership and individually injured partner can bring a direct action against the breaching partner and an accounting action.
Feb. 2017 Essay 5	**Agency** Defining the agency relationship. Agents: scope of authority; actual, inherent, and apparent authority. Power of agent to bind the principal: • Liability to third party when agent enters into a contract with a third party on behalf of a disclosed principal on terms not authorized by the principal. • Liability to third party when agent enters into a contract with a third party on behalf of an undisclosed principal on terms authorized by the principal but the principal later repudiates the contract.

Exam Date & Question	Business Associations: Agency and Partnership
	• Liability to third party when agent enters into a contract on behalf of a partially disclosed principal for goods different from those authorized by the principal and the principal accepts the goods.
Feb. 2018 Essay 6	**Partnership** Partner's right to dissolve an at-will partnership. Partner's continuing duties to the partnership during the winding-up process. Partner's fiduciary duties to the partnership and other parties during the winding-up process; duty not to appropriate partnership opportunities during the winding-up of the partnership business.

Business Associations: Corporations and Limited Liability Companies

Exam Date & Question	Business Associations: Corporations and Limited Liability Companies
Feb. 2005 Essay 1	**Corporations** Officer's authority: power of president to hire attorney to initiate action on behalf of corporation (to collect accounts receivable). Authority of corporate officers: acts within scope of ordinary course of business. Authority of board of directors: declaration of dividends, acts in extraordinary course of business.
July 2005 Essay 2	**Corporations** Promoter liability for pre-incorporation contract; promoter as agent in establishing corporation. Novation. Factual issue whether promoter would be personally liable based on whether company intended to held promoter liable: can be argued either way. Corporation's ratification or adoption of pre-incorporation contract: express and implied adoption.
Feb. 2006 Essay 5	**Corporations** Authority of board of directors to call a special meeting of shareholders. What constitutes proper notice for a special shareholder meeting.

Exam Date & Question	Business Associations: Corporations and Limited Liability Companies
	Voting rights of different classes of stock: conditions imposed on voting rights by articles of incorporation. Proxy agreements: definition; requirements for a proper appointment. Quorum requirements: majority needed to dissolve corporation.
July 2006 Essay 5	**Corporations** Breach of fiduciary duty of majority shareholder for failure to disclose material information to minority shareholders; what constitutes material information. Duty of care and business judgment rule in approving a merger. Duty of fair dealing when a majority shareholder purchases the interest of the minority shareholders.
July 2007 Essay 9	**Corporations and LLCs** Members' right (of a manager-managed LLC) to maintain an action against manager of LLC for mismanagement: derivative action vs. direct action. Procedural requirements for bringing a derivative action (set forth in ULLCA). Members of LLC right to bring a derivative action on behalf of LLC for mismanagement.

Exam Date & Question	Business Associations: Corporations and Limited Liability Companies
	What constitutes a violation of manager's fiduciary duty of care: negligence standards; simple negligence, gross negligence. Business judgment rule. Personal liability of LLC members for negligence. Piercing the LLC veil to hold members personally liable: "mere instrumentality" or "unity of interest and ownership."
Feb. 2008 Essay 5	Corporations Corporate officer and director's duty of loyalty to corporation. Safe harbors for director who breaches his duty of loyalty: approval by disinterested directors, approval by disinterested shareholders, or fairness (RMBCA). Duty of board of directors to act on an informed basis when reviewing a contract in which a director has an interest. Business judgment rule; duty of care.
Feb. 2009 Essay 9	Corporations When directors are entitled to the protection of the business judgment rule. Directors' duty to become informed before making business decisions. Breach of duty of care; breach of duty of loyalty. Director's failure to disclose his interest in a transaction to the other directors.

Exam Date & Question	Business Associations: Corporations and Limited Liability Companies
	Exculpatory provisions in articles of incorporation shielding directors from liability in money damages for failure to exercise adequate care in performance of their duties as directors.
Feb. 2010 **Essay 5**	Corporations Closely held corporation. Shareholder's right of inspection of corporation's books and records (proper purpose of valuing shares of corporation). Shareholder's right to dividends; whether a suit to compel payment of a dividend is a suit to enforce a right of the corporation or a suit to enforce an individual right of the shareholder. Business judgment rule.
July 2010 **Essay 9**	Corporations Shareholder voting: importance of "record date" for determining voting eligibility. Proxy agreements: definition and revocability, action inconsistent with a proxy. Shareholder of record may vote at shareholder's meeting. Whether a corporation has the right to vote treasury shares. Whether certificate of incorporation or by-laws control when there is a conflict.
Feb. 2011 **Essay 7**	Corporations Filing of articles of incorporation: sets effective date of corporate existence.

Exam Date & Question	Business Associations: Corporations and Limited Liability Companies
	Liability of persons purporting to act on behalf of corporation with knowledge that articles of incorporation have not been filed. Personal liability by those who purport to act for a corporation if they entered the contract with knowledge there was no incorporation.
Feb. 2012 Essay 9	**Corporations** Notice requirements for special meeting of directors (stating the purpose of meeting not necessary): waiver of notice by a director by attending and voting. Quorum required for action at special meeting of board of directors. What it means to be "legally present" at a meeting: all directors must be able to simultaneously hear all others who are present.
July 2012 Essay 8	**Corporations and LLCs** Member-managed LLC; whether majority member of member-managed LLC has fiduciary duties that require it to bring claims against an LLC member. Claim of LLC v. claim of individual member of LLC. When a derivative action in a member-managed LLC may be brought. Involuntary dissolution: "oppression doctrine" as applied to LLC.

Exam Date & Question	Business Associations: Corporations and Limited Liability Companies
	Limited liability of LLC members and managers: piercing the LLC veil.
July 2013 Essay 6	**Corporations and LLCs** Member-managed LLC: members in a fiduciary relationship with duty of utmost trust and loyalty. Where member participates in a competing business but the express terms of the operating agreement allow members to have such an interest ("opting-out" of the duty of loyalty). Liability of members for debts of LLC: improper dissolution and winding up of LLC; notice to creditors. Piercing the LLC veil: "alter ego" where factors are considered: improper use of the LLC form, siphoning funds, intermingling personal and business funds, failure to follow corporate accounting formalities.
July 2014 Essay 6	**Corporations** Whether shareholders have authority to amend corporation's bylaws and if so, what are proper matters (e.g., procedures for nominating directors). Shareholders' power to amend or repeal board-approved bylaws. Derivative suit: to vindicate corporate rights; must make demand on the board. Ability of shareholders to bring direct suit: to vindicate shareholder's own rights.

Exam Date & Question	Business Associations: Corporations and Limited Liability Companies
July 2015 Essay 4	**Corporations** Director's conflicting interest transaction/director self-dealing. Business judgment rule. Safe harbor for director who breaches his duty of loyalty: approval by disinterested directors, approval by disinterested shareholders, or fairness (RMBCA). Corporate directors' breach of duty of loyalty where unable to show that the transaction was fair to the corporation even if not properly authorized. Corporate directors' breach of duty of care by failure to be adequately informed prior to decision-making.
July 2016 Essay 1	**Limited Liability Companies** Determining whether an LLC is member-managed or manager-managed when its certificate of organization and operating agreement are silent. Whether a member in a member-managed LLC had actual or apparent authority to bind the LLC to a contract based on determinations of whether the acts were within the ordinary course of the LLC's activities or outside it. Consequences of an LLC member's withdrawal: constitutes a "dissociation" and not a "dissolution" and winding up of the business.

Exam Date & Question	Business Associations: Corporations and Limited Liability Companies
Feb. 2017 Essay 4	**Corporations** Shareholder's right to inspect accounting records and board minutes if there is a "proper purpose"; proper purpose as a shareholder includes trying to determine whether improper corporate transactions have occurred. Shareholder has burden to show credible evidence of possible mismanagement to obtain inspection of books and records. When the board can seek dismissal of a shareholder's derivative suit: need for good faith, reasonable inquiry by majority of board's qualified directors into the shareholder's allegations. Fiduciary and good faith duties of directors; when the business judgment rule protects directors' conduct.
July 2018 Essay 6	**Corporations and LLCs** Determining when a corporation comes into existence: filing of articles of incorporation. Personal liability on a contract by a party acting on behalf of a corporation when she did not know that the business had not been properly incorporated. Limited liability in cases of defective incorporation: "de facto corporation" and "corporation by estoppel" doctrine. Personal liability of inactive investor in the business on an employment contract; apply

Exam Date & Question	Business Associations: Corporations and Limited Liability Companies
	defective-incorporation principles, de facto corporation, and corporation by estoppel doctrines.

Civil Procedure

Exam Date & Question	Civil Procedure
Feb. 2005 **Essay 3**	**Civil Procedure** Jurisdiction: federal subject matter jurisdiction based on diversity of citizenship (28 U.S.C. § 1332(a)); diversity established at the time the suit is filed. Aggregation of claims to satisfy the amount-in-controversy requirement. Federal courts' basis for supplemental jurisdiction under 28 U.S.C. § 1367(a) over all claims that "derive from a common nucleus of operative fact." Venue: change of venue under 28 U.S.C. § 1404(a) is only permitted to a court where the action could have been brought originally (i.e., where venue was proper at the time suit was filed).
July 2005 **Essay 6**	**Civil Procedure** Standard for granting TRO under FRCP 65(b) (to enjoin employee from violating the non-compete provision in contract and disclosing trade secrets). Standard for granting preliminary injunction: (1) risk of "irreparable harm" to plaintiff if preliminary injunction is not granted; (2) likelihood of plaintiff's success on the merits of the underlying claim; (3) "balance of the equities"—likelihood that the harm the plaintiff

Exam Date & Question	Civil Procedure
	will suffer in the absence of the preliminary injunction outweighs the harm the defendant will suffer if it is granted; (4) the public interest. A mandatory injunction: order compelling party to engage in particular acts.
Feb. 2006 Essay 3	**Civil Procedure** Jurisdiction: federal subject matter jurisdiction based on anticipation of a federal defense; "well-pleaded complaint rule." Jurisdiction: federal subject matter jurisdiction based on diversity of citizenship (28 U.S.C. § 1332(a): determining domicile based on residence and "intent to remain." FRCP 4(k)(1): asserting personal jurisdiction over a non-resident defendant. Exercise of state's long-arm statute where it extends jurisdiction as far as the Due Process Clause of the 14th Amendment allows; evaluation of internet-based contacts.
July 2006 Essay 6	Civil Procedure Amended pleadings: complaint may be amended "once as a matter of course at any time before a responsive pleading is served" under FRCP 15(a) and will "relate back to the date of the original pleading" if requirements of FRCP 15(c) are met. Complaint amended after statute of limitations had run to correct a mistake in the name of a defendant.

Exam Date & Question	Civil Procedure
	Final judgment rule; consideration of statutory and judge-made exceptions, including the collateral order exception.
	FRCP 16(a) and (f): pre-trial conferences and court's power to sanction a party for party's attorney for failure to appear.
	Where entry of default judgment may be an abuse of discretion.
Feb. 2007 Essay 3	**Civil Procedure**
	Discovery: determining what is discoverable. Plaintiff served requests for production of documents in personal injury action seeking investigative and accident reports and the bus driver's entire personnel file, including safety and driving records and disciplinary records.
	FRCP 26 (b)(1): "documents relevant to a claim or defense."
	FRCP 26 (b)(3): materials "prepared in anticipation of litigation."
July 2007 Essay 2	**Civil Procedure**
	Removal from state court to federal court; determining citizenship of executor for diversity and removal purposes.
	Preclusive effect of default judgment when court had subject matter and personal jurisdiction.
	FRCP 13(a): compulsory counterclaim requirement.

Exam Date & Question	Civil Procedure
Feb. 2008 Essay 6	**Civil Procedure** FRCP 50(b): judgment as a matter of law ("JMOL", also called a judgment notwithstanding the verdict, "JNOV"); when the motion must be brought. FRCP 50(a): standard for granting a motion for JMOV. FRCP 59(b): procedure for filing a motion for a new trial and the "miscarriage of justice" standard for granting it. Juror misconduct: challenge based on bias and nondisclosure during *voir dire*.
July 2008 Essay 5	**Civil Procedure** FRCP 19: joinder of a "necessary party." FRCP 13(a): defendant's counterclaim against plaintiff is compulsory when it arises from the "same transaction or occurrence." Federal courts' basis for supplemental jurisdiction under 28 U.S.C. § 1367(a) over all claims that "derive from a common nucleus of operative fact" (unpaid $50 restaurant bill).
Feb. 2009 Essay 5	**Civil Procedure and Conflict of Laws** FRCP 4 and Due Process clause of U.S. Constitution: evaluating basis for email service of process on a foreign corporation. Action against a foreign corporation on federal law claim and state law claim.

Exam Date & Question	Civil Procedure
	Federal court sitting in diversity must apply choice-of-law rule of the state in which court sits when there is non-federal claim. Restatement (Second) of Conflict of Laws § 145: applying choice of law rules to an issue in tort (unfair competition).
July 2009 Essay 6	Civil Procedure Process for removing a case from state court to federal court. FRCP 20: joinder of claims in "same transaction or occurrence" and "common questions of law and fact." Subject matter jurisdiction. Diversity jurisdiction. Supplemental jurisdiction statute 28 U.S.C. § 1367; claims arising out of state law; "common nucleus of operative fact" test.
Feb. 2010 Essay 6	Civil Procedure Subject matter jurisdiction. Jurisdiction: federal subject matter jurisdiction based on diversity of citizenship and amount-in-controversy requirement (28 U.S.C. § 1332(a)). Determining citizenship of corporation and permanent resident alien for diversity purposes. Diversity jurisdiction in breach of contract case (insurance policy). Domestic relations exception to federal courts' exercise of diversity jurisdiction: federal courts

Exam Date & Question	Civil Procedure
	will not exercise jurisdiction over cases that are primarily marital disputes. FRCP 20: joinder of claims in "same transaction or occurrence" and "common questions of law and fact"; the logical-relationship test.
July 2010 Essay 7	Civil Procedure FRCP 4(k)(1): asserting personal jurisdiction over a non-resident defendant. Exercise of state's long-arm statute where it extends jurisdiction as far as the Due Process Clause of the 14th Amendment allows; evaluation of contacts with forum state for finding of specific jurisdiction based on nonresident's purposeful availment of benefits of forum state and foreseeability of being haled into court. Jurisdiction: federal subject matter jurisdiction based on diversity of citizenship and amount-in-controversy requirement (28 U.S.C. § 1332(a)). Determining citizenship of corporation for diversity purposes. Determining domicile based on residence and "intent to remain"; satisfying the amount-in-controversy requirement. Determining whether federal-question jurisdiction exists: whether claims alleged in complaint are created by federal or state law (federal statute, but state law claim).

Exam Date & Question	Civil Procedure
Feb. 2011 **Essay 8**	**Civil Procedure** FRCP 12(b)(6): motion to dismiss for failure to state a cause of action. FRCP 12(b): failure to join other defenses: waiver of defense of insufficient service of process when motion challenging service not joined in initial Rule 12(b) motion. FRCP 13(g): defendant's answer may state crossclaim against a co-defendant where the claim arises out of the same transaction or occurrence that is the subject matter of the original action. Whether federal court has independent subject matter jurisdiction over a state law cross-claim where there is no diversity of citizenship and the amount-in-controversy is not satisfied. Federal courts' basis for supplemental jurisdiction under 28 U.S.C. § 1367(a) over all claims that "derive from a common nucleus of operative fact."
July 2011 **Essay 5**	**Civil Procedure** Determining what is an appealable final judgment. FRCP 54(b): final judgments are immediately appealable when there is "no just reason for delay." Final judgment rule; consideration of the collateral order exception (non-appealable

Exam Date & Question	Civil Procedure
	interlocutory order regarding forum-selection clause). Whether pendant appellate jurisdiction would apply to allow appellate court to hear appeal where party is seeking review of a non-final order.
Feb. 2012 Essay 7	**Civil Procedure and Conflict of Laws** When removal from state court to federal court is proper under 28 U.S.C. § 1441(a). Venue: change of venue under 28 U.S.C. § 1404(a) permitted to a court where the action could have been brought originally, convenience of the parties, and "interest of justice." Application of *Erie* Rule following a change of venue: court to which the case is transferred must apply the same law as would have been applied by the original court: change of venue does not affect the law to be applied.
July 2012 Essay 7	**Civil Procedure** FRCP 15(a)(2): leave to amend its answer based on facts learned in discovery where defendant previously failed to raise the affirmative defense. Defendant's burden to plead affirmative defenses under FRCP 8(c). FRCP 56(a): standard for grant of summary judgment: "no genuine issue as to any material fact"; in considering the evidence, inferences

Exam Date & Question	Civil Procedure
	must be drawn most favorable to the party opposing the motion.
Feb. 2013 Essay 5	**Civil Procedure** Claim preclusion (*res judicata*): determining issues of privity between parties (family relationship). Issue preclusion (*collateral estoppel*): effect of privity on non-party's ability to present her claim in a second suit even if it is factually related to claims and defenses presented in first suit. Non-mutual issue preclusion: abandonment of "traditional" requirement of mutuality where the party asserting issue preclusion and party against whom it was asserted were both bound by the prior judgment.
July 2013 Essay 1	**Civil Procedure** Jurisdiction: federal subject matter jurisdiction based on diversity of citizenship (28 U.S.C. § 1332(a)). Determining domicile: residence and "intent to remain." Determining citizenship for corporations: dual citizenship based on state where incorporated and where corp. has its principal place of business ("nerve center" test). Venue: basis for venue when jurisdiction is based on diversity (28 U.S.C. § 1391(b)).

Exam Date & Question	Civil Procedure
	Obtaining personal jurisdiction over a corporate defendant (FRCP 4(k)). Exercise of state's long-arm statute where it extends jurisdiction as far as Due Process Clause of the 14th Amendment allows.
Feb. 2014 Essay 4	**Civil Procedure** FRCP 26(b)(1), FRCP 34(a)(1). Discovery: work product rule: whether a document prepared in the course of a contract dispute is non-discoverable "work product" when the document was not prepared in anticipation of litigation. Discovery; destruction of discoverable materials, deletion of potentially relevant emails when litigation is possible, role of routine document retention/destruction policy. Duty to preserve discoverable materials when litigation is anticipated. Determining appropriate sanctions for spoliation of evidence: court considers the level of culpability of the spoliating party and the degree of prejudice the loss of evidence causes the other party.
July 2014 Essay 4	**Civil Procedure** FRCP 24(a): intervention as a matter of right; identification of the three requirements for intervention of right. Standard and requirements for granting TRO under FRCP 65(b).

Exam Date & Question	Civil Procedure
	Standard for granting preliminary injunction: (1) risk of "irreparable harm" to plaintiff if preliminary injunction is not granted; (2) likelihood of plaintiff's success on the merits of the underlying claim; (3) "balance of the equities"—likelihood that the harm the plaintiff will suffer in the absence of the preliminary injunction outweighs the harm the defendant will suffer if it is granted; (4) the public interest.
Feb. 2015 Essay 5	**Civil Procedure** FRCP 4 (h): service of process on a corporation. Subject matter jurisdiction based on federal question (sexual harassment and sex discrimination claim). Subject matter jurisdiction over third party complaint for state law claim, breach of contract: based on diversity, Determining corporate citizenship for purposes of diversity. Determining domicile and amount-in-controversy requirement. FRCP 14(a): impleader rules, improper joinder of claims, third-party claim based on derivative liability.
July 2015 Essay 2	**Civil Procedure** FRCP (4)(k)(1)(A): asserting personal jurisdiction over a non-resident defendant. Exercise of state's long-arm statute where it extends jurisdiction as far as the Due Process

Exam Date & Question	Civil Procedure
	Clause of the 14th Amendment allows; evaluation of contacts with a forum state. Jurisdiction: 28 U.S.C. § 1331: original jurisdiction, cause of action based on violating a federal statute. Jurisdiction: 28 U.S.C. § 1367: supplemental jurisdiction, "same case or controversy" even though based on contract claim or state claim.
July 2016 Essay 6	**Civil Procedure** FRCP 4(k)(1)(A): transient jurisdiction: personal jurisdiction based on service of process of defendant who is physically present in the state. Jurisdiction: 28 U.S.C. § 1331: subject matter jurisdiction; federal question jurisdiction based on a federal statute. Jurisdiction: diversity jurisdiction (lack of diversity) 28 U.S.C. § 1332 over state-law negligence claim. Jurisdiction: 28 U.S.C. § 1367: supplemental jurisdiction, "same case or controversy" over a negligence or state claim. Venue: Determining appropriate venue under 28 U.S.C. § 1391(b).
July 2017 Essay 6	**Civil Procedure and Conflict of Laws** FRCP 12—whether a motion to dismiss can be amended prior to a responsive filing (no prejudice or delay to other party) to add a ground for dismissal that would have been

Exam Date & Question	Civil Procedure
	waived because it was not raised in the initial Rule 12(b)(6) motion to dismiss. FRCP 4(e): insufficient service of process when documents are not personally served but delivered to parents' home where defendant used to live. Choice-of-law rules: a federal court sitting in diversity applies the choice-of-law rules of the state where the federal court sits (Restatement) and according to a signed contract between the parties.
Feb. 2018 Essay 5	**Civil Procedure** FRCP 11: filing an answer with a general denial of factual and legal contentions where the attorney made no inquiry into the facts before doing so. Procedure for presenting a Rule 11 motion: giving attorney an opportunity to correct the pleading. Court's discretion in imposing sanctions; possible sanctions; on whom sanctions may be imposed: the party, the attorney the law firm.

Constitutional Law

Exam Date & Question	Constitutional Law
July 2008 **Essay 2**	**Constitutional Law** First Amendment: freedom of speech. Defamation: public figure, "actual malice", "reckless disregard" of the truth. Freedom of the press: lack of immunity for breaking the law or committing a tort. Invasion of privacy: lawfully obtained information involving a matter of public concern, reasonable expectation of privacy.
July 2009 **Essay 2**	**Constitutional Law** First Amendment: freedom of speech. Sedition Statute: inciting illegal conduct must meet "imminent and likely" test under *Brandenburg.* Abusive Words Statute: "fighting words" are unprotected speech when likely to cause a violent reaction. Statutes may be overbroad where it punishes speech that is merely rude or abusive because it reaches protected speech. Commentary on matters of public concern are afforded the highest level of First Amendment protection.

Exam Date & Question	Constitutional Law
July 2010 Essay 4	**Constitutional Law** First Amendment and types of forums: public forum, limited public forum and nonpublic forum. Public forum: content-neutral regulation must meet intermediate scrutiny (statute preventing leaflet distribution on a public street). Limited public forum: rules applicable to traditional public forum apply; no exception to requirement of content neutrality when religious speech is at issue. Non-public forum: state can regulate conduct without communicative value in a nonpublic forum.
July 2011 Essay 8	**Constitutional Law** Equal Protection Clause of the Fourteenth Amendment. Gender-based discrimination: separate nursing facilities and programs based on gender. State action doctrine: when can actions of private party be considered state action. Classification based on gender: assessed under heightened or intermediate scrutiny. State must show important governmental objectives and means employed are substantially related to achievement of those objectives. Remedying past discrimination as an "important governmental objective."

Exam Date & Question	Constitutional Law
July 2012 **Essay 3**	**Constitutional Law** Interstate Commerce Clause: Congressional authority to regulate economic activities that have a "substantial economic effect" on interstate commerce (Federal statute against workplace violence). 10th Amendment: federalism, Congress may regulate public and private actors on the same terms. Bar of the 11th Amendment: when abrogation of state immunity is satisfied.
Feb. 2013 **Essay 3**	**Constitutional Law** First Amendment: freedom of speech (refusal to recite pledge of allegiance). State action where private actor exercises a "public function (running a privately owned "company town"). First Amendment ban on compelled expression; compelled expression of a political belief (school required students to salute flag and Pledge Allegiance). Regulation of student speech by schools and teachers. Traditional public forum: content-neutral regulation of speech, intermediate scrutiny of a statute (preventing leaflet distribution).

Exam Date & Question	Constitutional Law
Feb. 2014 Essay 1	**Constitutional Law** Fifth Amendment: city ordinance requiring business to install floodlights is not a *per se* taking. Unconstitutional regulatory taking of property without unjust compensation compared to regulating with a legitimate state interest. Determining a regulatory taking: three-part balancing test under *Penn Central*. Exaction of an easement to obtain a building permit, uncompensated taking, *Dolan* test.
Feb. 2015 Essay 2	**Constitutional Law** Age-based discrimination: rational basis scrutiny. Equal Protection Clause of the Fourteenth Amendment: three levels of scrutiny for EP claims. Scope of congressional authority under Section Five of Fourteenth Amendment.
Feb. 2016 Essay 4	**Constitutional Law** Commerce Clause: state statute that applies equally to in-state and out-of-state utilities. Where a state statute treats in-state electricity consumers more favorably than out-of-state consumers. Where state acts as a "market participant."

Exam Date & Question	Constitutional Law
July 2017 **Essay 2**	**Constitutional Law** State's sovereign immunity under the 11th Amendment from suit for damages in federal court. *Ex parte Young:* suit against State's Superintendent of Banking to enjoin enforcement of allegedly unconstitutional statute not barred by 11th Amendment when it is an official-capacity action and seeks prospective relief. Dormant commerce clause: balancing test is used when the state law is nondiscriminatory on its face (because it applies equally to local and out-of-state banks) but still imposes an incidental burden on interstate commerce.
July 2018 **Essay 1**	**Constitutional Law** Whether a federal act requiring state officers/ agencies to assist in the enforcement of federal drug laws violates fundamental principles of federalism. Concepts of federalism and dual sovereignty. Constitutional exercise of Congress's spending power when it conditions the granting of federal funds on a state's compliance with "federal statutory and administrative directives.

Contracts

Exam Date & Question	Contracts
July 2007 **Essay 1**	**Contracts** Requirements for an enforceable contract: offer, acceptance, consideration and, when required, a signed writing. Requirements for an offer; distinguishing between a counteroffer and an inquiry. Rules for acceptance: when is acceptance effective upon dispatch, the "mailbox rule"; rejection effective upon receipt. Rule where an acceptance is sent after a rejection: the one to reach the recipient first is effective. Statute of Frauds: one-year provision. Personal services contract: damages are available but specific performance is not.
July 2008 **Essay 8**	**Contracts** Calculating damages in breach of contract: cost-of-completion v. difference in value. Award of consequential damages: test of foreseeability. Damages must be calculable with reasonable certainty to be recoverable (calculation difficulties with respect to a new business). Calculation of damage award includes subtraction of costs avoided by not having to perform; reduction of award to present value

Exam Date & Question	Contracts
	when assessing damages based on loss of future income; duty to mitigate damages.
July 2009 Essay 5	**Contracts** Consideration: requirement of a "bargained-for exchange." Past consideration or past performance. Substitutes for consideration: material benefit rule (moral consideration) and promissory estoppel.
July 2010 Essay 2	**Contracts/Article 2** UCC Article 2 sale of goods. Breach of warranty—creation of express warranty through affirmations of fact relating to the goods that are part of the basis of the bargain. Misrepresentation as common law basis to avoid or rescind the contract; common law principles supplement the Code under UCC § 1-103. Revocation of acceptance; duty to inspect and difficulty of discovery of latent defects. Damages: recovery of contract price and incidental and consequential damages; alternative remedy of "cover" damages.
Feb. 2011 Essay 6	**Contracts** Offer to modify an existing contract: process of offer, counteroffer, acceptance. Breach of contract: failure to use good faith efforts to obtain loan which was a condition precedent to party's duty to perform.

Exam Date & Question	Contracts
	Recovery of expectation damages, including loss of potential investment when foreseeable at time of contract. Punitive damages not recoverable in contract.
Feb. 2012 Essay 3	**Contracts** Substantial performance; when failure to perform or defective performance amounts to a material breach. Determining when a contract is divisible to allow some measure of recovery in event of breach; when a party may be entitled to restitution based on part performance.
Feb. 2013 Essay 2	**Contracts/Article 2** UCC Article 2 sale of goods. Reasonable grounds for insecurity regarding prospective performance; written demand for adequate assurances; when failure to provide such assurances constitutes a repudiation. Retracting a repudiation.
July 2013 Essay 7	**Contracts/Article 2** UCC Article 2 sale of goods. Statute of frauds: sale of goods over $500. Application of "merchant confirmatory memo" exception. What constitutes a signature to satisfy the statute of frauds. Where statute of frauds is not satisfied but the contract is valid in other respects, it is

Exam Date & Question	Contracts
	enforceable as to the goods that have received and accepted.
July 2014 Essay 2	**Contracts/Article 2** Consideration: modification and pre-existing duty rule. Exception under the Restatement (Second) for changed circumstances that were unanticipated at the time of contract and the modification would be fair and equitable. UCC Article 2: consideration not required for modifications made in good faith. Defense of economic duress/business compulsion: when a threat of non-performance is "wrongful" or "improper."
July 2015 Essay 3	**Contracts/Article 2** Statute of frauds: sale of goods over $500, oral agreement followed by a signed letter indicating that the contract exists. Repudiation of contract, attempted retraction of repudiation. Damages: difference between contract price and resale price plus incidental damages.
July 2016 Essay 5	**Contracts** Whether contract rights may be assigned without the obligor's consent when the assignment does not change the obligor's duty in any material respect. What is required for an effective assignment.

Exam Date & Question	Contracts
	The assignee's rights to enforce the contract when the obligor does not perform. Determining third-party beneficiary status: differences between incidental vs. intended beneficiaries. Delegation of duties: where obligor remains liable for any breach by the delegate.
Feb. 2017 Essay 1	**Contracts/Article 2** Offer formation under the Code; whether a party is a merchant. Irrevocable offers; "firm offers." Output contracts.
Feb. 2018 Essay 3	**Contracts/Article 2** Determining whether UCC Article 2 or the common law applies under a mixed contract: predominant purpose test. Applicability of the parol evidence rule to a prior oral agreement. Consideration: modification and pre-existing duty rule.
July 2018 Essay 2	**Contracts/Article 2** Determining whether UCC Article 2 applies to a transaction involving a lawnmower. Offer; rejection; renewing an offer. Promise to keep an offer open: by common law, by statute, by reliance. Terminating the power of acceptance: indirect revocation.

Criminal Law and Procedure

Exam Date & Question	Criminal Law and Procedure
July 2007 **Essay 5**	**Criminal Law** Second-degree murder (shot friend while aiming at lamp behind friend). *Mens rea*, "malice aforethought", "depraved-heart" murder. "Extreme indifference to value of human life", reckless behavior. Causation: defendant's acts must be both the actual ("but for") and proximate cause of death. A "dependent intervening cause", a consequence of defendant's prior wrongful conduct, breaks the chain of causation when it is bizarre or out of the ordinary.
Feb. 2008 **Essay 8**	**Criminal Law and Procedure** Fourth Amendment: determining a "seizure" and whether that seizure was reasonable under the Fourth Amendment. Exclusionary rule and "fruit of the poisonous tree." Questioning of suspect when there is a "reasonable articulable suspicion." *Miranda* rights: determining when they attach (suspect is subject to an in-custody interrogation). When is a subject "in custody." Voluntary confession compared to an involuntary confession.

Exam Date & Question	Criminal Law and Procedure
July 2009 **Essay 7**	**Criminal Law and Procedure** Fourth Amendment: standing to challenge the legality of a search, reasonable expectation of privacy. Attempted robbery: elements, intention & actions "beyond mere preparation." Defense of voluntary withdrawal or abandonment of crime when actions go beyond mere preparation.
July 2010 **Essay 8**	**Criminal Law** Larceny by false pretenses: elements. *Actus reus* and *mens rea* elements of false pretenses. False statements of a material fact compared to commercial puffery. False statements made knowingly with the intent to defraud.
July 2011 **Essay 2**	**Criminal Law and Procedure** Fourth Amendment: whether constitutional reasonableness of a traffic stop depends on the motivation of the officer. Probable cause to stop vehicle based on minor traffic violation. Search and seizure; evidence found in "plain view." *Miranda* rights: determining when they attach (arrested and being questioned).

Exam Date & Question	Criminal Law and Procedure
	Whether *Miranda* violation's taint's subsequent interrogation. *Miranda* rights: demand for an attorney must be unequivocal and unambiguous as compared to defendant's statement: "Maybe I need a lawyer."
July 2012 Essay 2	**Criminal Law** Involuntary manslaughter: elements. *Mens rea* required for involuntary manslaughter liability; varies by jurisdiction recklessness, gross, criminal, or culpable negligence (defendant dumped bags of marbles at traffic intersection at night resulting in car accident and passenger death). Causation: causation in fact (but for cause) proximate cause. Accomplice liability on charge of involuntary manslaughter: elements. Must have *mens rea* required for underlying offense.
Feb. 2014 Essay 5	**Criminal Law and Procedure** Fifth Amendment: double jeopardy, two crimes with different elements, theft and burglary. Due Process Clause requires the prosecution to prove all elements of offense beyond a reasonable doubt: jury instructions which create either an "irrebutable conclusive presumption" or a "rebuttable presumption" unconstitutionally shift burden of proof to the defendant.

Exam Date & Question	Criminal Law and Procedure
	Sixth Amendment: right to jury trial on element of offense, where the value of stolen goods may increase the penalty for a crime, said value is a question for the jury and must be proved beyond a reasonable doubt.
July 2014 Essay 1	**Criminal Law and Procedure** Sixth Amendment right to counsel: is charge–or offense–specific; does not attach to uncharged crimes where there is no formal adversarial judicial proceeding. *Miranda* rights: demand for an attorney must be unequivocal and unambiguous as compared to defendant's statement: "I think I want my lawyer here before I talk to you." *Miranda* rights: standard for waiver of rights is voluntary, knowing, and intelligent.
July 2015 Essay 5	**Criminal Law** Affirmative defense: requirements to establish defense of not guilty by reason of insanity (NGRI). Manslaughter: elements; *actus reus and mens rea* (death caused by the criminal operation of a motor vehicle). Affirmative defense: duress (knife held to throat of the defendant).
Feb. 2018 Essay 2	**Criminal Law** Determining whether a criminal defendant is competent to stand trial.

Exam Date & Question	Criminal Law and Procedure
	If found competent and the prosecution proceeds, whether a jurisdiction that follows the *M'Naughten* test should find the defendant not guilty by reason of insanity (NGRI).

Evidence

Exam Date & Question	Evidence
Feb. 2008 Essay 4	**Evidence** Hearsay; exceptions to hearsay. Business-records exception; statements made for purpose of receiving medical diagnosis or treatment. Two evidentiary privileges applicable to the marital relationship: testimonial spousal privilege and marital confidential communications privilege. Hearsay admissible to impeach hearsay declarant's credibility.
Feb. 2009 Essay 2	**Evidence** FRE 404: character evidence. Impeachment of witness on cross-examination with a specific instance of prior bad act about lying on job application. FRE 608(b): forbids use of extrinsic evidence to impeach witness's character for truthfulness. FRE 612: only counsel for opposing party can offer document to refresh recollection of a witness.
Feb. 2010 Essay 7	**Evidence** Admissibility of relevant evidence in negligence action. FRE 701: non-expert opinion evidence.

Exam Date & Question	Evidence
	FRE 404(a): evidence of character trait not admissible for proving action in conformity on a particular occasion. FRE 406: habit evidence (cell phone usage). Relevancy of memory loss concerning events related to the incident. FRE 401-403: where parties have stipulated to injuries, evidence of additional injuries not mentioned in stipulation are inadmissible as waste of time and may be unfairly prejudicial.
Feb. 2011 Essay 2	Evidence Impeaching witness credibility with a prior inconsistent statement. Extrinsic evidence admissible to impeach credibility between prior out-of-court statement and witness's trial testimony. FRE 801(d)(1)(C): non-hearsay statement of identification. FRE 801(d)(1)(A): a prior inconsistent statement admissible as not hearsay when the statement is made under oath, under penalty of perjury at trial, hearing, proceeding, or deposition. FRE 405(a): admissibility of evidence of good character of a relevant character trait may be introduced by defendant only through reputation or opinion testimony.

Exam Date & Question	Evidence
Feb. 2012 Essay 1	**Evidence** FRE 401: relevant evidence. FRE 407: subsequent remedial measures (hospital change in policy). FRE 408: settlement offers of disputed claim. FRE 409: offers to pay medical expenses. FRE 412(a): "Rape Shield" rule. FRE 412(b)(2): in civil cases, otherwise inadmissible evidence of allege victim's sexual behavior is admissible "if its probative value substantially outweighs the danger of harm to any victim."
Feb. 2013 Essay 7	**Evidence** FRE 401: relevant evidence. Hearsay: text message is a "written assertion." FRE 803(1): hearsay exception for present sense impressions. FRE 803(6): text message as a business record. "Thumbs-up" as a non-verbal assertion made out-of-court: when hearsay and when not.
July 2013 Essay 4	**Evidence** Hearsay; exceptions to hearsay (911 call). FRE 803 (1): present sense impressions. FRE 803 (2): "excited utterances." FRE 803 (4): "statements made for medical diagnosis and treatment."

Exam Date & Question	Evidence
	Sixth Amendment Confrontation Clause: whether the statement to police was testimonial.
July 2014 Essay 5	**Evidence** Impeachment of witnesses with evidence of prior convictions and specific instances of misconduct (felony drug conviction, perjury, sexual assault). FRE 609(a): evidence of prior convictions admissible to attack witness's character for truthfulness. FRE 609(b): determining the 10-year time limit for admissibility: limit runs from date of conviction or release from confinement whichever is later. Admissibility of evidence subject to FRE 403 balancing test. FRE 608(b): cross-examination of witness about specific instance of prior non-conviction misconduct (lying on job application and resume). FRE 608(b): forbids use of extrinsic evidence to impeach witness's character for truthfulness.
Feb. 2016 Essay 2	**Evidence** Hearsay; exceptions to hearsay. FRE 803 (1): present sense impressions. FRE 803 (2): "excited utterances." Sixth Amendment Confrontation Clause: whether the statement was testimonial (arguments either way in this case).

Exam Date & Question	Evidence
	FRE 801(d)(1)(C): admissibility of out-of-court statement of identification testified to at trial. Character evidence: inadmissible to show propensity.
July 2016 Essay 2	**Evidence/Criminal Procedure** *Miranda* rights: whether defendant's crying is a testimonial communication. Hearsay; exceptions to hearsay, non-hearsay. FRE 803(5): recorded recollections. FRE 801(d)(2): non-hearsay (statement of opposing party). FRE 803(5): even if written notes meet exception to be read into evidence, admissible as an exhibit only if offered by the adverse party. Whether post-invocation statements are admissible when custodial suspect initiates communication with police: fresh set of Miranda warnings required. Police obligation to honor an invocation of *Miranda* right to counsel terminates 14 days after suspect has been released from interrogative custody (*Maryland v. Shatzer*).
July 2017 Essay 5	**Evidence** FRE 401: relevant evidence. Hearsay, non-hearsay, and exceptions to hearsay. Hearsay: when an out-of-court statement is not hearsay.

Exam Date & Question	Evidence
	Whether criminal defendant's admission violates *Miranda* when the police officer's question was limited to weapons and asked after a shooting (public safety exception to *Miranda*).
	Non-hearsay: statement of opposing party.
	Hearsay exceptions: custodian describing what he heard around the time of the incident:
	• FRE 803 (1): hearsay exception: present sense impressions; or
	• FRE 803 (2): "excited utterances."
July 2018 Essay 5	Evidence
	Admissibility of relevant evidence.
	Opinion evidence: lay and expert opinion.
	Hearsay; business-records exception.
	Physician-patient privilege; patient's waiver of the privilege by filing a civil lawsuit placing her medical condition "in issue."
	Non-hearsay: statement by an opposing party.
	Hearsay exception for statements made for medical diagnosis or treatment.
	Question of whether roommate's texting behavior is evidence of habit or character.

Family Law

Exam Date & Question	Family Law
Feb. 2005 Essay 4	**Family Law and Conflict of laws** Standards governing custodial parent's relocation: balancing of impact on visitation by noncustodial parent against benefits of the move for the child; "best interests of the child." Enforceability of a registered child support order in a non-issuing state pursuant to the Uniform Interstate Family Support Act (UIFSA). Interstate enforcement and modification of child support orders (UIFSA). Interstate modification of child custody order as governed by Parental Kidnapping Prevention Act (PKPA) and the Uniform Child Custody Jurisdiction and Enforcement Act (UCCJEA).
July 2005 Essay 4	**Family Law** Whether statute of limitations in state's paternity statute violates unwed biological father's substantive due process rights under 14th Amendment. Factors for establishing a significant parental relationship. Presumption of paternity; presumption of legitimacy. Nonparent estopped from disclaiming parental responsibilities when previously consented to act as a parent and support child and child's

Exam Date & Question	Family Law
	interests would be harmed by terminating the parental relationship. Interpreting a state visitation statue: violation of due process of parent when no deference is given to fit parent's determination of best interests of child.
Feb. 2006 Essay 4	**Family Law** Annulment: whether spouse can reinstate alimony/spousal maintenance from previous marriage when her second marriage is annulled. Grounds for annulment: fraud is basis for annulment if goes to the "essentials of the marriage"; asset value is not generally considered an "essential." Validity of marriage: where there is a subsequent marriage before divorce decree is final, public policy favors finding a valid marriage. "Marriage-saving" doctrines: presumption of validity of subsequent marriage and removal of the impediment to marriage.
July 2006 Essay 4	**Family Law and Conflict of Laws** Validity of common law marriage in states that do not recognize common law marriages. Requirements to establish a common law marriage. Whether agreements between cohabitants establish property or support rights ("ceremony of commitment").

Exam Date & Question	Family Law
	Protection under the due process clause of 14th Amendment for unwed father who lived with his child for a substantial portion of his child's life and wishes to maintain an active, custodial relationship with the child; his parental rights cannot be severed without his consent or showing of parental unfitness.
Feb. 2007 Essay 4	**Family Law and Conflict of Laws** Jurisdiction and divorce: over the marriage and over the property. A court's jurisdiction to grant its domiciliary's divorce petition as long as the state's jurisdictional requirements are satisfied. Divisible divorce: a court's jurisdiction in an *ex parte* divorce extends to the marriage only and not to the property of the marriage. Personal jurisdiction over both spouses needed for property division order. No-fault divorce granted based on separation and irreconcilable differences; does not matter whether the separation was nonconsensual or one spouse is seeking to reconcile. Separate property and marital property.
July 2007 Essay 3	Family Law Basis for setting aside or modifying a divorce settlement or agreement before a final divorce judgment is entered: when a spouse's coercive behavior, fraud, or duress results in a substantively unfair agreement.

Exam Date & Question	Family Law
	Setting aside a divorce settlement agreement based on serious misconduct by the mediator. Factors for determining spousal maintenance award: contributions to marriage, duration of marriage, parties' financial resources and needs.
Feb. 2008 Essay 3	**Family Law** Meaning of an adoption order; whether an adoptive parent can dissolve the adoption when the parent quarrels frequently with the child. Seeking a retroactive modification of child support obligation: forbidden by federal law. Voluntary reduction of income not a basis to obtain downward modification of child support obligation unless made in good faith and without incurring hardship on child. Must show a "substantial change in circumstances" to obtain modification of future support obligation. Support of children of employable age; compliance with reasonable parental demands.
July 2008 Essay 7	**Family Law and Conflict of Laws** Which state law determines enforceability of a premarital agreement: law of state where contract is signed or law of state with which parties have the "most significant relationship." Determining enforceability of premarital agreement governing property distribution: voluntariness, unconscionability, reasonable disclosure of assets and liabilities.

Exam Date & Question	Family Law
	Premarital agreement regarding child support or custody is unenforceable if it is not in the "best interests of the child."
	Separate and marital property; in a majority of states, marital property continues to accrue until final divorce decree.
Feb. 2009 Essay 8	**Family Law**
	Due process requirements for assertion of personal jurisdiction over a nonresident parent in a child support action.
	State long-arm statute in fact pattern same as in Uniform Interstate Family Support Act (UIFSA).
	Contract to waive Dad's child support duty unenforceable because inconsistent with "best interest of child."
	Calculation of child support based upon income and earnings of parents, not public assistance levels.
	Child custody and visitation determination, "best interest of child" standard.
July 2009 Essay 3	**Family Law**
	Interstate enforcement and modification of child support orders (Uniform Interstate Family Support Act (UIFSA).
	Enforcement of registered child support order in non-issuing state even when non-issuing state lacks personal jurisdiction over respondent (UIFSA).

Exam Date & Question	Family Law
	Under federal Parental Kidnapping Prevention Act (PKPA), only issuing jurisdiction can modify child custody order so long as child or any contestant continues to reside in that state and issuing states does not decline to exercise jurisdiction.
	Custody modification based on a "substantial change in circumstances": whether parental relocation qualifies as such a change; consideration of "best interests of the child."
	Modification of child support obligation; may not be modified retroactively, but may be modified prospectively if there is a "substantial change in circumstances" that significantly reduces the child's need or the obligor's ability to pay.
Feb. 2010 Essay 3	**Family Law** Basis for setting aside a settlement agreement before a final divorce judgment is entered: if fraud, overreaching, or duress results in a substantively unfair agreement. Consideration of marital misconduct in property or alimony determination; distinction between marital misconduct and financial misconduct in award considerations. Marital and separate property: professional license (law degree is marital property only in NY) acquired during the course of the marriage.

Exam Date & Question	Family Law
	Rehabilitative award for spousal support and maintenance; factors in determining spousal support and maintenance (alimony) awards.
July 2010 Essay 6	Family Law Determining enforceability of premarital agreement governing property distribution: voluntariness, unconscionability, reasonable disclosure of assets and liabilities. Marital and separate property: property acquired during marriage and by gift; pension can be part marital and part separate property. Alimony: financial resources, marital contributions and marital duration, spousal misconduct, injured spouse.
Feb. 2011 Essay 5	Family Law Basis for invalidating a separation agreement's property and support provisions: unconscionability or fraud; whether misrepresentation of paternity would support a finding a fraud. Whether a property division award can be modified after divorce decree is entered. Modification of spousal-support award and a "substantial change in circumstances." Modification of child-support obligation based on non-paternity.

Exam Date & Question	Family Law
July 2011 Essay 6	Family Law and Conflict of Laws Validity of common law marriage in states that do not recognize common law marriages. Requirements to establish a common law marriage. Substantive due process rights under 14th Amendment of unwed biological father. Whether state can permit adoption without the consent of the biological father. Determining a child's "home state" under the Uniform Child Custody Jurisdiction and Enforcement Act to issue an initial custody decree (UCCJEA).
July 2012 Essay 4	Family Law Which state has jurisdiction to issue a child custody decree when the child has no "home state": pursuant to the Uniform Child Custody Jurisdiction and Enforcement Act, state may exercise jurisdiction based on "significant connections" and "substantial evidence" (UCCJEA). Weight given to older child's wishes or preferences in determining custody: relevant but not determinative. Interpreting a state grandparent child-custody statute: violation of due process of parent when no deference is given to fit parent's determination of best interests of child.

Exam Date & Question	Family Law
July 2013 Essay 3	**Family Law** Whether a court would order a parent to stop making contributions from her earnings to a religious organization. Court intervention in parental disputes: whether a court would require one parent to follow the other's preference with respect to child rearing practices (allowing daughter to take skating lessons). Court intervention when health or safety of child is at issue because of parent's religious belief; court may order medication given to child. Whether court may deny a parent custody based the parent's religious faith based on a threat to the child's health or safety: "best interests of the child."
July 2014 Essay 3	**Family Law** Interstate enforcement and modification of child support orders (UIFSA), personal jurisdiction, subject matter jurisdiction, enforcement in non-issuing state. UIFSA: does not govern property distributions in divorce decree. Modification of child support obligation, retroactive modification, prospective support obligation and "substantial change in circumstances", involuntary loss of income or voluntary loss of income.

Exam Date & Question	Family Law
	Modification of property-division award in divorce decree, personal jurisdiction and property division.
Feb. 2016 Essay 6	**Family Law** Determining enforceability of premarital agreement under the Uniform Premarital Agreement Act (UPAA): voluntariness, unconscionability, reasonable disclosure of assets and liabilities. Determination of marital property and separate property; principles of equitable distribution; winning lottery ticket purchased before divorce filing.
Feb. 2017 Essay 3	**Family Law and Conflict of Laws** Requirements to establish a common law marriage. Recognition of common law marriage in other states. Determination of marital property; principles of equitable distribution. Putative-spouse doctrine. Illegality of bigamy: when a first marriage is not legally dissolved, a second marriage has no legal effect. Presumption that the latest in a series of marriages is valid: designed to protect parties' expectations but may be rebutted.

Exam Date & Question	Family Law
	Property and support rights between unmarried co-habitants based on an express or implied contract to share assets. Fundamental right of parents to control the upbringing of their children; a fit parent is presumed to act in the best interests of her children. Determining non-parent's visitation rights.
Feb. 2018 Essay 1	**Family Law** Enforceability of premarital agreement with property division, alimony, and child custody provisions. Divisibility of marital assets at divorce: separate and marital property. Whether a parent's adulterous conduct is considered by the court in making a custody decision. "Best interests of the child": factors in determining child custody.

Real Property

Exam Date & Question	Real Property
July 2007 **Essay 6**	**Real Property** Requirements for a valid deed (grantee must be identified). Adverse possession: elements. Adverse possessor's claim to possession against subsequent BFP. State recording statute and its effect on owner who acquired land by adverse possession (where owner had no deed to record).
July 2008 **Essay 4**	**Real Property** Landlord/tenant: creating periodic and at-will tenancies. Statute of Frauds: one-year provision (3 years in some jurisdictions). Violation of statute of frauds, possession of property and acceptance of rent, creation of at-will or periodic tenancy, month-to month tenancy. Terminating at-will and periodic tenancies: notice requirements. Assignment of lease that is silent about assignments, liability for rent of assignor and assignee.
Feb. 2009 **Essay 4**	**Real Property** Tenancy in common: statutory presumption when conveyance to 2 or more grantees.

Exam Date & Question	Real Property
	Joint tenancy: 4 unities test (common law); is a joint tenancy or tenancy-in-common created when a deed's language includes "jointly" and "equally, to share and share equally" but does not mention survivorship? Act and consequence of severing a joint tenancy: mortgage by one joint tenant, contract to sell by one joint tenant. Distinction between "lien theory" and "title theory" jurisdictions. Bona fide purchaser for value; recording of mortgagee gives constructive notice to purchasers regardless of unrecorded deed. Doctrine of equitable conversion.
Feb. 2010 Essay 2	**Real Property** Types of easements. Actual notice, constructive notice, or inquiry notice with regard to easements which are visible (power lines) and easements which are not visible (underground gas lines), when the easements are not recorded and when there are subsequent purchasers for value. "Shelter doctrine." Conveyance by full covenant and warranty deed: covenant against encumbrances.

Exam Date & Question	Real Property
July 2010 **Essay 5**	**Real Property** Terms of conveyance ambiguous: fee simple on condition subsequent or fee simple determinable and the consequences that arise from each. Interpreting grantor's intent: preference for fee simple on condition subsequent. Future interest and interpreting a state statute which allows interest to pass by will; interpreting a will with a survivorship contingency of "my surviving children" where one child predeceases testator.
July 2011 **Essay 4**	**Real Property** Termination of easement: abandonment, non-use, and intent to abandon. Common law first-in-time, first-in-right principle. Notice-type state recording statute that has a grantor-grantee index. Actual, constructive, or inquiry notice. "Wild deed": deed recorded outside the chain of title and therefore undiscoverable by a reasonable search of the grantor-grantee index; provides no constructive notice to subsequent purchaser. Easement (visible railroad tracks): subsequent purchaser put on inquiry notice.

Exam Date & Question	Real Property
Feb. 2012 **Essay 8**	**Real Property** Appurtenant easement extinguished by merger with a subsequent deed. Creation of easement by implication (implied from prior use): identify criteria. Distribution of proceeds in foreclosure sale with multiple lenders when the first loan which was recorded is a construction loan or "future-advance" mortgage. Whether future-advances mortgage payments are required or optional determines the rights of junior lender.
Feb. 2013 **Essay 1**	**Real Property** Landlord/tenant: commercial lease with term-of-years. Constructive eviction: elements at common law. No implied duty for landlord to repair leased premises under common law; courts reluctant to imply duty to repair in commercial leases. Written lease contained no term requiring landlord to repair the air-conditioning. Covenant of quiet enjoyment does not include duty to repair. Surrender of a lease by tenant and whether the landlord accepted the surrender (retaining keys) or held the tenant to lease terms.

Exam Date & Question	Real Property
	Common law rule: landlord had not duty to mitigate damages and not entitled to recover unpaid future rents, only what was in arrears at time of suit. Other courts allow landlords to sue tenants for wrongful termination and seek damages equal to difference between unpaid rent due and fair market rental value or other valuations for unpaid future rent.
July 2013 Essay 8	**Real Property** New home construction: implied warranty against latent defects, implied warranty of fitness, implied warranty of habitability (rejection of caveat emptor doctrine). Extension of implied warranty of latent defects to remote grantees or subsequent purchasers in most jurisdictions (despite lack of privity with builder). Assumption of mortgage: express assumption required for personal liability on unpaid mortgage obligation; implied assumption of mortgage. Quitclaim deeds: contain no warranties of title.
Feb. 2015 Essay 4	**Real Property** Adverse possession: elements, calculating the 10-year statutory period by tacking of time of previous possessors. Title acquired by adverse possession extends to only occupied portion and not entire parcel of land.

Exam Date & Question	Real Property
	Warranty deed: 6 covenants, present and future covenants, breach of covenant of seisin.
	Easement: buyer taking property subject to existing sewer-line easement.
Feb. 2017 Essay 6	**Real Property** Landlord/tenant.
	Validity of lease provision requiring landlord's written consent for assignment; whether refusal to consent to assignment must be reasonable.
	Actions constituting an abandonment of the premises.
	Landlord's options when tenant abandons: accept surrender of the premises; re-let or attempt to re-let the premises, and leave the premises vacant and sue tenant for unpaid rent.
	Landlord's duty to mitigate.
Feb. 2018 Essay 4	**Real Property** Whether there was a breach of a warranty deed's title covenants, specifically, the covenant against encumbrances.
	Whether damages are available for breach of the covenant against encumbrances when the easement was plain and obvious and if so, what they would be.
	Whether there was a breach of the implied warranty of habitability.

Exam Date & Question	Real Property
July 2018 Essay 3	**Real Property** Application of the nonconforming-use doctrine: whether proposed changes to expand a convenience store are exempt from the zoning ordinance as a nonconforming use depends on whether they are substantial or unsubstantial changes. "Future-advances" loan: whether the bank's commitment to make future advances optional or obligatory. Determining whether a bank's mortgage has priority over a mechanic's lien when the mortgage was recorded and payment was made before the filing of the lien.

Secured Transactions

Exam Date & Question	Secured Transactions
Feb. 2005 Essay 6	**UCC Article 9**
	Unperfected security interest compared to judicial lien creditor.
	Purchase-money security interest; definition of "goods"; delayed filing and 20-day grace period after delivery of the collateral to perfect by filing, and security interest relating back to the date of the attachment.
	Item of sale changing from "goods" to a "fixture" (an oven).
	Priority of liens: competing security interests, judgment liens, mortgages, "fixture filing."
July 2005 Essay 3	**UCC Article 9**
	Attachment and rights of creditors with unperfected security interests.
	Creditor's use of self-help remedies to repossess and sell collateral.
	Foreclosure sale: notice requirement to debtor and "any secondary obligor"; guarantor of loan with actual knowledge of sale but who did not receive proper notice of the sale.
	Deficiency judgments: secured party fails to comply with foreclosure rules in business transactions, there is a deficiency, and the "rebuttable presumption rule."

Exam Date & Question	Secured Transactions
Feb. 2006 **Essay 6**	**UCC Article 9** Consignment agreement: where consignor retains title to goods. Collateral in inventory: creditor of a consignee "deemed to have rights and title to goods identical" to those of consignor. Purchase-money security interest in inventory held by a consignor of goods. Priority of liens: competing security interests. Perfection of a security interest; financing statement; notification requirements.
July 2006 **Essay 7**	**UCC Article 9** Improper disposition of the collateral (consumer goods); public v. private disposition of collateral; "commercially reasonable" manner; notice of sale. Remedies of consumer as a result of secured party's failure to provide notice of disposition and a "commercially reasonable" disposition of collateral; actual damages, statutory damages, right of redemption, Deficiency judgments: secured party fails to comply with foreclosure rules in a consumer transaction, liability of the debtor, "absolute bar" rule, and "rebuttable presumption rule."
Feb. 2007 **Essay 7**	**UCC Article 9** Perfection of a security interest in accounts receivable.

Exam Date & Question	Secured Transactions
	Errors in UCC filing statements: ineffective filing of financing statement where the name of debtor is incorrect (trade name as opposed to the name of the corporation), "seriously misleading" test", search of records would not disclose the financing statement. Automatic perfection of security interest in accounts (upon attachment); when assignment of accounts do not transfer "significant part of assignor's outstanding accounts." Priority of liens: competing security interests and "first to file or perfect rule."
Feb. 2008 Essay 7	**UCC Article 9** Perfection of a security interest in deposit or demand accounts: secured party must have control of the account to perfect their interest. Errors in UCC finance statements; effective filing of financing statement where the name of debtor was incorrect; "seriously misleading" test; search of records would disclose financing statement. Priority of liens: competing security interests.
July 2008 Essay 1	**UCC Article 9** Perfection of a security interest; inventory and equipment; after acquired collateral. Motor vehicles: certificate of title statute and notation on certificate of title as perfection of a security interest as compared to filing a financing statement.

Exam Date & Question	Secured Transactions
	Priority of liens: competing security interests. Continuation of security interest: accessions, priority rules governing accessions with certificate of title statutes; description of the collateral in creditor's security agreement. Purchase-money security interest in equipment takes priority over competing security interest which was acquired earlier in time.
July 2009 Essay 4	**UCC Article 9** Security interest in equipment; after acquired collateral. Agreement that is called a lease may be a security interest: "economic realities" of the transaction where lessee has option to become owner with a nominal payment at end of the lease. Perfection of a security interest. Creditor's use of self-help remedies to repossess and sell collateral. Priority of liens: competing security interests. Applying proceeds of sale towards competing interests. Good faith purchaser of collateral at foreclosure sale: "transferee for value."
Feb. 2010 Essay 1	**UCC Article 9** Security interest in inventory. Retention of title by seller of delivered goods until payment is made is ineffective, resulting in

Exam Date & Question	Secured Transactions
	an unperfected security interest in goods rather than a retention of title.
	Perfecting a security interest in inventory: raw materials as inventory.
	Priority of liens: competing security interests, perfected v. unperfected.
	Attachment of security interest, debtor must have "rights in collateral" (undelivered goods.)
Feb. 2011 Essay 3	UCC Article 9
	Security interest in inventory.
	Sale of collateral: no continuation of security interest with a buyer in ordinary course of business (BIOCOB), consumer.
	Purchase-money security interest in consumer goods and perfected security interest without filing of financing statement; subsequent sale of collateral.
July 2011 Essay 1	**UCC Article 9**
	Security interest in inventory and equipment including future or after acquired items.
	Perfection of a security interest.
	Retention of title by seller of delivered goods until payment is made is ineffective and results in an unperfected security interest in goods rather than the retention of title; seller must file a financing statement or retaining possession of goods to perfect a security interest.
	Priority of liens: competing security interests.

Exam Date & Question	Secured Transactions
	Agreement that is called a lease may be a security interest: "economic realities" of the transaction where lessee becomes the owner after making all payments.
July 2012 Essay 5	**UCC Article 9** Perfection of a security interest: present and future inventory, equipment not included. Sale of collateral: no continuation of security interest with a buyer in ordinary course of business (BIOCOB), consumer. Security interest extending beyond inventory to equipment when inventory is traded for equipment. Retention of title by seller of delivered goods until payment is made is ineffective and results in an unperfected security interest in goods rather than the retention of title; seller must file a financing statement or retain possession of goods to perfect a security interest. Priority of liens: competing security interests and a judgment lien.
Feb. 2013 Essay 4	**UCC Article 9** Perfection of a security interest: "purchase-money security interest" in consumer goods without a financing statement. Sale of collateral and continuation of security interest with a buyer who is not a buyer in the ordinary course of business (BIOCOB), but rather

Exam Date & Question	Secured Transactions
	is a buyer of goods used for "personal, family or household purposes." Gift of collateral, for no value and the continuation of a security interest.
Feb. 2014 Essay 3	**UCC Article 9** Security interest in equipment including future or after acquired items. Priority of liens: competing security interests and "first to file-or-perfect rule." Filing financing statement before security agreement or loan is obtained, attachment, and determining the date of perfection. Sale of collateral and continuation of security interest in equipment where buyer is not a buyer in ordinary course of business (BIOCOB) because seller is not in the business of selling goods of that kind.
Feb. 2015 Essay 3	**UCC Article 9** Criteria for a valid security interest. Security interest in "accounts" and "inventory." Classifying property as an account, inventory, or equipment. Inventory: raw materials as inventory, items left for repair by customers are not inventory. Sale of collateral: no continuation of security interest with a buyer in ordinary course of business (BIOCOB), consumer to consumer.

Exam Date & Question	Secured Transactions
	Priority of liens: competing security interest and a judgment lien.
Feb. 2016 Essay 1	**UCC Article 9** Security interest in "present and future inventory" in a store; buyer in ordinary course of business (BIOCOB) and "shelter principle" affecting subsequent transfers. Perfection of retailer's security interest: "purchase-money security interest" in "consumer goods"; retailer retaining title is in effect a security interest. Sale of collateral: no continuation of security interest with a buyer in ordinary course of business (BIOCOB), consumer to consumer. Security interests in proceeds (check) of sale of collateral.
July 2016 Essay 4	**UCC Article 9/Real Property** Remedies available to a secured creditor when debtor defaults on "equipment"; whether "self-help" is available. Security interest in equipment: defining "equipment" under Article 9. Perfection of a security interest in equipment including fixtures. Determining the priority of interests in equipment after it becomes a fixture when a bank holds a mortgage on the real property; exception relating to the priority of a "purchase-

Exam Date & Question	Secured Transactions
	money security interest" in fixtures as against an encumbrance of the related real property. "Fixture filing."
July 2017 Essay 3	**UCC Article 9** Perfection of a security interest in "present and future accounts." UCC Article 9 criteria for attachment of a security interest. Priority of liens: competing security interests and "first to file or perfect rule." Determining priority of interests between perfected and unperfected interests. Discharge of obligations by account debtors to assignee upon receiving notice of the assignment.

Torts

Exam Date & Question	Torts
Feb. 2008 **Essay 2**	**Torts** Strict products liability (food poisoning): liability of commercial product sellers compared to occasional, non-commercial food seller. Defective products: where a product's risk of being unreasonably dangerous cannot be eliminated, adequate warnings or instructions are required or the product is defective. Negligence: where there are multiple defendants and cannot show which of three parties acted negligently because parties acted independently and not jointly. Where *res ipsa loquitur*, alternative liability, and joint enterprise liability are unavailable to support a negligence claim.
Feb. 2009 **Essay 7**	Torts Negligence: standard of care owed by tenant to tenant's guest; standard for 8-year old child. Contributory negligence/comparative negligence. Negligence *per se*, state statute to keep apartment in good repair. Causation, proximate cause of injuries, intervening causes to break chain of causation.

Exam Date & Question	Torts
Feb. 2010 **Essay 4**	**Torts** Battery: intent and knowledge to a substantial certainty (pedestrian hit by a baseball that traveled over fence at baseball stadium). Negligence. Vicarious liability of employer for negligence of employee. Custom: industry standards in profession in determining negligence. "Eggshell skull."
Feb. 2011 **Essay 4**	**Torts** Battery: prima facie case, intent to cause a harmful or offensive contact (use of stun gun). Whether frisk as part of routine screening process is "offensive." Defense to battery: consent. Strict products liability: manufacturing defect. "Eggshell skull."
Feb. 2012 **Essay 4**	**Torts** False imprisonment: elements (refusal to restart a ferris wheel) Vicarious liability of employer for acts of employee. Negligence: standard of care. Whether parent can bring claim for emotional distress: "zone of danger"; contemporaneously observe injury to child.

Exam Date & Question	Torts
July 2012 Essay 6	Torts Negligence: duty of care owed by university to its students; causation (failure to repair broken lock). No general duty to come to aid of another: exception if increase in harm and reliance on actor. Duty of psychotherapist: to warn a reasonably identifiable individual of credible threat from patient; no duty to an indeterminate class. "Eggshell skull."
July 2013 Essay 2	Torts Vicarious liability of employer for acts of employee committed within the scope of employment. Principal's liability for agent's torts based on apparent authority of employee. Negligence: causation.
February 2015 Essay 1	Torts Independent contractor vs. employee Vicarious liability of employer for acts of employee committed within the scope of employment. Negligence *per se:* violation of traffic ordinance (double-parking). Whether conforming to custom is a defense to negligence.

Exam Date & Question	Torts
	Indemnification of employer by employee for tort claim.
July 2015 Essay 1	Torts Negligence: minor engaged in a hazardous, adult activity (snowmobiling). Standard of care owed by landowner to a trespasser and to a licensee. Attractive nuisance doctrine. No general duty to come to aid of another: exception if increase in harm and reliance on actor. Contributory/comparative negligence.
July 2016 Essay 3	Torts Medical malpractice: standard of care for the relevant specialty and medical community. Negligence. Strict products liability (pesticide in herbal tea); manufacturing defect. Implied warranty of merchantability. Causation requirement not met where multiple product manufacturers and plaintiff cannot link any particular defendant to his injury. Strict products liability claim against commercial seller.
July 2017 Essay 1	Torts Strict products liability: whether public fireworks display is an abnormally dangerous activity.

Exam Date & Question	Torts
	Negligence; negligence *per se*. Burden of taking precautions compared to risk of harm. Assessing proximate cause: danger invites rescue. Vicarious liability: whether one who employs an independent contractor is liable for harm caused by the independent contractor when the contractor is hired to engage in work involving a special danger to others and the employer knows about such danger.

Trusts and Estates: Decedents' Estates

Exam Date & Question	Trusts and Estates: Decedents' Estates
Feb. 2005 Essay 5	**Decedents' Estates** Revocation: physical destruction with intent to revoke; multiple copies of will executed while only 1 copy was destroyed; proponent's burden of proof. Revival of will: destruction of will revives prior will pursuant to state revival statute. Codicil: handwriting and changing a bequest on a previously executed will. Execution requirements: doctrine of dependent relative revocation. Rule of ademption: specific bequest of real property no longer in testator's estate at time of death and whether there is entitlement to replacement property.
July 2005 Essay 1	**Decedents' Estates** Whether a life insurance beneficiary be changed by a will provision. Joint bank account with right of survivorship; account of convenience, power to write checks only and the intent of the testator. Lapsed legacy: death of beneficiary prior to death of testator, state lapse statute, application of statute to class gifts and to persons who died before will was executed.

Exam Date & Question	Trusts and Estates: Decedents' Estates
	Uniform Probate Code (UPC) anti-lapse statute compared to common law and state lapse statutes.
Feb. 2006 Essay 7	**Decedents' Estates** Advancement: whether inter vivos gift by donor is an advancement on the beneficiary's legacy; intention of the testator. Slayer statute: felonious intent and killing of decedent compared to negligence as cause of testator's death. Intestacy distribution incorporated in will. Per capita distribution of assets compared to per stirpes distribution of assets.
July 2006 Essay 3	**Decedents' Estates** When a joint will constitutes a will contract: determined by language used, "each of us agrees" is a contract between husband and wife; contract becomes irrevocable at death of first spouse; includes property acquired after death of a spouse; beneficiaries of joint will as contract creditors of surviving spouse's estate. Doctrine of "facts of independent significance" and rule of construction that wills "speak at the time of death." Incorporation by reference: document executed after will executed as compared to a document in existence prior to the execution of a will; invalid bequest not evidenced by a testamentary instrument.

Exam Date & Question	Trusts and Estates: Decedents' Estates
Feb. 2007 Essay 5	**Decedents' Estates** Effect of a stock dividend or stock split on a specific bequest of "my 100 shares"; common law compared to the Uniform Probate Code (UPC). Disclaimer of legacy: sister of testator disclaims: beneficiary deemed to have failed to survive testator, lapsed legacy, anti-lapse statute. Advancement: whether the inter vivos gift by donor is an advancement on the beneficiary's legacy; intention of the testator. Abatement of legacies in order of the classification of legacy.
Feb. 2008 Essay 1	**Decedents' Estates** Grounds for contesting a will: elements for undue influence. Effect of finding of undue influence: can invalidate all or a portion of the will. Rules of intestacy are followed upon invalidation of a will. When a residuary bequest fails, does the invalidated share pass to the testator's heirs or to the remaining residuary legatees: common law approach—"no residue of residue" rule (testator's heirs) compared to UPC approach—"residue of residue" rule (other residuary legatee)

Exam Date & Question	Trusts and Estates: Decedents' Estates
February 2009 Essay 3	**Decedents' Estates** Distribution of assets in will. Effect of stock dividend or stock split on a specific bequest of "my 100 shares." Rule of ademption: specific bequest of real property no longer in testator's estate at time of death, replacement property. Generically described property in a will, "my automobile" does not follow rule of ademption when a different car is owned at time of death. Disclaimer of legacy: friend disclaims and beneficiary deemed to have failed to survive the testator, lapsed legacy, anti-lapse statute.
July 2009 Essay 9	**Decedents' Estates** Grounds for contesting a will: elements for undue influence, elements for fraud in the execution (misrepresents character/contents of the instrument) and in the inducement. Effect of finding of undue influence: can invalidate all or a portion of the will. General power of appointment and the proper exercise of power; residuary clause in will that makes no mention of power of appointment. Simultaneous Death Act: common accident where beneficiary survives testator by 1 week. Intestacy distribution rules: whether testator's niece or testator's uncle take if will is declared invalid. Parentelic method (UPC approach) of determining heirship compared to intestacy

Exam Date & Question	Trusts and Estates: Decedents' Estates
	schemes governed by the civil law consanguinity method (minority method).
July 2010 **Essay 3**	**Decedents' Estates** Execution requirements of a will: doctrine of integration for multi-page will (validity when all pages of will are together but unstapled). Codicil: effect of handwritten change to bequest on a previously executed will. Doctrine of dependent relative revocation (revocation based on mistaken assumption of law or fact is ineffective if testator would not have revoked if he had accurate information). Bequest to "my children" when testator intended only biological children to take under the will; rights of adopted and non-marital child. Reformation of a will: use of extrinsic evidence to correct a mistake.
Feb. 2011 **Essay 9**	**Decedents' Estates** Execution requirements of a will: handwritten wills that are properly executed compared to holographic wills. Whether a life insurance beneficiary be changed by a will provision. Incorporation by reference of memorandum regarding testator's jewelry located in safe deposit box.

Exam Date & Question	Trusts and Estates: Decedents' Estates
	Lapsed legacy and anti-lapse statute with respect to a husband that predeceases the testator. Abatement of legacies in order of the classification of legacy.
Feb. 2012 Essay 5	**Decedents' Estates** Execution requirements of will. Codicil: cannot republish a will that has not been properly executed; codicil will act as a valid partial will. Incorporation by reference where testator says "I republish my will": specific identification to the earlier document and testator's intent to incorporate the document. Intestacy distribution rules: "slayer statute" where heir murdered another but did not kill testator. Rule of ademption: specific bequest of real property no longer in testator's estate at time of death; common law ademption compared to "intent test" regarding substitute or replacement property. Effect of a stock dividend or stock split on a specific bequest of "my 400 shares."
July 2012 Essay 9	**Decedents' Estates and Conflict of Laws** Conflict of laws: domicile and distribution of personal property, real property and law of the situs.

Exam Date & Question	Trusts and Estates: Decedents' Estates
	Holographic wills and interpretation of two different state statutes with different execution requirements where both statutes find the will invalid—all assets to pass intestate.
	Interpretation of two different state intestacy statutes with regard to inheritance rights of biological, adopted, and non-marital child when paternity has been established; constitutional standards.
July 2013 Essay 9	**Decedents' Estates**
	Prenuptial agreement: waiving rights in spouse's estate will not preclude a surviving spouse from inheriting from a will that was executed after the prenuptial agreement was signed.
	Divorce: when parties have only filed for divorce as compared to a final divorce at the time of the testator's death.
	Adopted-out child: rights to inherit when child is adopted out by a family member.
	Appointment of personal representative when will is silent; priority of devisees.
Feb. 2015 Essay 6	**Decedents' Estates**
	Revocation of will or a portion of a will: testamentary intention to revoke and physical act; writing on will to "call lawyer to fix" is only intent to have will reviewed, not revoked.
	Rights of after-born child (pretermitted child) not mentioned in will.

Exam Date & Question	Trusts and Estates: Decedents' Estates
	Distribution of assets of revocable trust: interpreting state intestacy statute and state statute regarding "illusory" revocable trusts (created during marriage).
Feb. 2016 Essay 5	**Decedents' Estates** Agent's authority to act under a durable health-care power of attorney (POA). Protection of agent from civil (wrongful death action) and criminal liability when acting in good faith. "Slayer statute": where one who intentionally caused the decedent's death is barred from sharing in the estate with regard to health care POA.
July 2017 Essay 4	**Decedent's Estates/Future Interests** Execution requirements of will. Validity of will when witnessed by an interested witness and effect on the bequest to that witness. Codicil: republication-by-codicil doctrine cures defect in previously validly executed will with interested witness problem. Bequest of household goods (furniture) made in an unattested document (memo) written after the will was executed and the will evidences intent to so dispose of the property. Whether a bequest violates the Rule Against Perpetuities (RAP).

Exam Date & Question	Trusts and Estates: Decedents' Estates
	Vesting of a class gift for purposes of the RAP when the class is closed and all members of the class have met any conditions precedent.

Trusts and Estates: Trusts and Future Interests

Exam Date & Question	Trusts and Estates: Trusts and Future Interests
July 2005 Essay 7	**Trusts and Future Interests** Testamentary trust. Elements of a valid trust: definite beneficiaries required; trust established to give income to "my friends" invalid for want of definite beneficiaries. Donee's exercise of special power of appointment to appoint trust assets (principal) and to create more limited interests (life estate). Special power of appointment exercised in favor of an impermissible object. Partially ineffective exercise of special power of appointment and consequences to permissible object.
Feb. 2006 Essay 1	**Trusts and Future Interests** Elements of a valid trust: trustee, beneficiary, and trust property. Revocable trust. Trust written on a napkin with intention to fund it at a later date: trust arises when funded. Pour-over will to a trust where the trust's terms were incorporated in a writing (napkin) that was written before the will. Incorporation by reference doctrine: testamentary additions to revocable trust.

Exam Date & Question	Trusts and Estates: Trusts and Future Interests
	Self-settled trusts; enforceability of spendthrift provision; reach by settlor's creditors to trust assets of revocable trust.
Feb. 2007 Essay 2	**Trusts and Future Interests** Testamentary trust. Elements of a valid trust: a trust established to give income to "my friends" fails because it lacks definite beneficiaries. Distribution of trust income to residuary legatee when trust fails; whether to accumulate trust income for ultimate distribution to remainder beneficiaries or currently distribute income to presumptive remainder beneficiaries. Creditor's right to reach trust income when trust contains no spendthrift provision. Rights of creditors no greater than rights of beneficiary. Bequest to charity that no longer exits: cy pres doctrine, general charitable intent.
July 2007 Essay 8	**Trusts** Drafting of trust agreement to reflect Settlor's intent. MEE task requires comparing list of Settlor's goals in creating the trust to the Trust Agreement drafted by the attorney and making changes to meet the Settlor's stated goals. Settlor wants full control of trust assets in memo: Settlor should retain power to revoke, to

Exam Date & Question	Trusts and Estates: Trusts and Future Interests
	withdraw principal; Settlor should be named as sole trustee.
	Trust should include an additions clause.
	Ascertainable standard for distributions of trust principal to wife and beneficiary's right to withdrawal of trust principal so that wife is comfortably provided for.
	Special testamentary power of appointment created by trust so that wife can reward her children in her will.
	Drafting using the term "issue" to ensure child that predeceases wife will take the deceased child's share of trust principal.
	Anti-lapse statutes and how they apply to inter vivos trusts as compared to testamentary trusts.
Feb. 2008 Essay 9	**Trusts** Irrevocable trust. Duties of trustee with respect to management of trust. Duty of loyalty: investing in a corporation where the trustee has a substantial investment. Duty to invest prudently: investing in closely held corporation that was "cash poor." Duty to diversify trust investments: investing 90% of trust assets in two corporations that were extremely similar and had same market risks. Duty of care: investing in items that did not earn income and were not liquid so income beneficiary received nothing and prevented

Exam Date & Question	Trusts and Estates: Trusts and Future Interests
	beneficiary from withdrawing trust principal as provided for in the terms of the trust.
July 2008 Essay 6	**Trusts** Revocable trust. Validity of pour-over will assets to a trust created during testator's lifetime either by testator or another. Validity of additions to revocable trust which was amended after will is executed. Incorporation-by-reference. Construction of a trust amendment with two possible interpretations: grantor's intent regarding age and survivorship contingencies. Whether grandchild is a substituted taker when trust instrument specifies "children" and includes words of survivorship ("who are living"). Anti-lapse statutes and application to wills as opposed to trusts.
July 2009 Essay 1	**Trusts** Irrevocable trust. Trustee with absolute and uncontrolled discretion to distribute income and principal; abuse of discretion by failing to distribute income based upon personal motives; disagreement with beneficiary's political opinions. Duty of loyalty: self-dealing; purchasing assets from the trust without court approval; no

Exam Date & Question	Trusts and Estates: Trusts and Future Interests
	appraisal but purchased by trustee at fair market value. Bequest to charity that no longer exists: *cy pres* doctrine, general charitable intent.
Feb. 2010 Essay 8	Trusts Revocable trust. After-born children: "surviving children" as a class does not close until Settlor's death and would include "after-born" children. Distribution of trust assets where remainderman predeceases the life tenant: follow the directives in trust instrument; outcome different under UPC where survivors take a predeceased person's share by representation. Disclaimer of interest in a trust by beneficiary: beneficiary deemed to predecease the Settlor; different result under UPC's survivorship rule. Trustee's duty to invest prudently. Duty of fiduciary of a revocable trust who is acting in accordance with Settlor's wishes as compared to the duty of a fiduciary of an irrevocable trust.
Feb. 2011 Essay 1	Trusts Trustee with uncontrolled discretion to distribute income and principal. Discretionary trust: rights of creditors no greater than rights of beneficiary to compel trustee to make payments.

Exam Date & Question	Trusts and Estates: Trusts and Future Interests
	Inheritance rights in trust of adopted grandchild who was adopted after testator's death.
	Where trust instrument creates a future interest in grandchildren: when does the class close.
	Vested remainder: trust provides that if the remainderman predeceases the life tenant that it shall pass to the child of the remainderman and the remainderman dies with no children; common law compared to UPC.
July 2011 Essay 3	**Trusts**
	Court's power to reform trust provisions: equitable deviation doctrine; reforming trust terms when there is an unanticipated change in circumstances (expanded under the Uniform Trust Code to include modification of administrative trust provisions as well as dispositive provisions).
	Bequest to charity that no longer exists, *cy pres* doctrine, presumption of general charitable intent under the UTC.
July 2012 Essay 1	**Trusts and Future Interests**
	Irrevocable trust.
	Termination of trust upon consent of the income beneficiaries and remainder beneficiaries if there is no material purpose yet to be performed.
	Whether limitation on remarriage of husband beneficiary is a material purpose.

Exam Date & Question	Trusts and Estates: Trusts and Future Interests
	Trust remainder to "Settlor's children": gift to a class related to a common ancestor with no condition of survivorship; who qualifies as trust remainder under common law as compared to a jurisdiction that adopted the UPC survivorship statute.
	"Surviving children" as a class of persons does not close until death of "Settlor" and includes children born after the creation of the trust (after-born).
	Trust termination: trust beneficiaries may direct distribution of trust property in any manner they choose and so direct the trustee.
Feb. 2013 Essay 8	**Trusts and Future Interests** Revocable trust (inter vivos); whether a revocable trust is amendable. Settlor's power of revocation includes the power to amend trust when trust is silent on power to amend or modify. Settlor's ability to amend trust without formalities necessary to execute a will (no need for witnesses to Settlor's signature). Revocable trust may be amended any time prior to Settlor's death and the amendment applies to assets conveyed to the trust in a pour-over will where the will was executed prior to amendment. Rule Against Perpetuities: interpreting the state statute provided in the MEE question; applying

Exam Date & Question	Trusts and Estates: Trusts and Future Interests
	common law rule to determine validity of Settlor's trust.
Feb. 2014 Essay 2	**Trusts and Future Interests** Testamentary trust. Determining what constitutes income and principal, sale of proceeds of real estate, rental proceeds, cash dividends, and stock dividends. Disclaimer made more than 9 months after testator's death is invalid pursuant to state statute; income beneficiary who invalidly disclaims is not deemed to have predeceased testator; common law rule allowing disclaimers at any time; acceleration of remainder not available where the remainder in will has survivorship contingency.
July 2015 Essay 6	**Trusts** Testamentary trust. Provision of trust that violates public policy is void (condition of marriage). Duty of loyalty: self-dealing, trustee purchasing stock from trust; trust beneficiaries may seek to rescission of the transaction or seek damages. Duty to invest trust assets in a prudent manner (mutual funds decline in value during economic downturn).

Exam Date & Question	Trusts and Estates: Trusts and Future Interests
Feb. 2017 Essay 2	**Trusts** Revocable trust. Settlor's power of revocation includes the power to amend trust when trust is silent on power to amend or modify. Under UTC, power to revoke or amend is exercisable by will unless the trust instrument provides otherwise. Power of appointment (specific not general) created in Settlor's trust and exercised in a subsequent will; "permissible appointees" compared to "impermissible appointees." Taker in default of ineffective appointment. Right of election. Surviving spouse's right to the elective share of probate assets pursuant to a state statute. Illusory transfer doctrine and fraudulent transfer doctrine (available in some jurisdictions) allowing surviving spouse to exercise the right of election to claim trust assets held in a revocable trust.
July 2018 Essay 4	**Trusts and Future Interests** Duties of trustee to the trust beneficiaries. Duty of loyalty: trustee rented a trust-owned apartment to himself but paid the market rate (self-dealing); "no-further-inquiry rule."

Exam Date & Question	Trusts and Estates: Trusts and Future Interests
	Duty of prudent administration (duty of care): trustee failed to purchase fire/casualty insurance on the trust's real property.

Duty to comply with applicable law: trustee allocated a $50,000 repair expense necessitated by a fire exclusively to income when it should have been allocated to principal.

Distribution of trust principal where the remainder interest was vested. |